HUMINTEL

THE SYNERGY OF HUMAN AND ARTIFICIAL INTELLIGENCE

"FROM FUN FACTS TO FUTURE VISIONS: THE POWERFUL FUSION OF HUMAN AND ARTIFICIAL INTELLIGENCE"

NITIN PANWAR

(AT THE FOREFRONT OF AI EVOLUTION AND DIGITAL TRANSFORMATION)

ISBN
Paperback 979-8-89588-636-6
Hardcase 979-8-89632-323-5

Contents

Personal Stories and Anecdotes: Author's Journey

Embracing the AI Revolution

From the moment I stepped into the world of artificial intelligence, I knew I was embarking on a remarkable journey. I vividly recall my first project—developing a predictive maintenance system. At first glance, it seemed like a straightforward task: minimize downtime and enhance efficiency. However, as I dove deeper, it quickly became clear that the true challenge lay in the intricacies of machine learning and data integration.

Working alongside a dynamic team that included data scientists, engineers, and industry experts was exhilarating. Each person brought a unique perspective, and together, we navigated the complexities of our project. I still remember the day we presented our initial model. It failed to deliver the insights we hoped for, which could have been disheartening. But rather than dwelling on the setback, we huddled together around a whiteboard, brainstorming fresh ideas. This spirit of collaboration turned a potential failure into an opportunity, leading us to innovative solutions that ultimately saved our organization significant costs.

The Heart of Collaboration

My experiences have taught me that the backbone of successful AI projects is collaboration. During another project, we focused on building an AI. This time, I collaborated with various departments, including customer support and IT, ensuring we fully understood the challenges faced by our users.

During the testing phase, we learned that while our bot was adept at answering common questions, it struggled with more complex inquiries. Instead of viewing this as a roadblock, we took it as a chance to enhance the bot's capabilities. We organized feedback sessions, and through iterative improvements, we created a chatbot that genuinely met our users' needs. This experience emphasized the importance of listening and adapting in AI development.

Facing Resistance Head-On

One theme that has come up repeatedly in my journey is the skepticism surrounding AI adoption. While working on a project to optimize supply chains, I encountered concerns from colleagues about potential job losses. Instead of brushing aside these fears, I took it upon myself to foster open dialogues.

I organized workshops that highlighted how AI could enhance roles rather than replace them. Sharing success stories from other organizations that had embraced AI was pivotal in shifting mindsets. I witnessed a transformation as my colleagues began to see AI as a partner, not a competitor. The discussions we had ignited enthusiasm and innovative ideas about how we could harness AI to streamline our workflows.

Learning Never Stops

In this fast-evolving field, continuous learning has become essential. I've attended numerous workshops and conferences, soaking in knowledge and insights from industry experts and fellow enthusiasts. One of the most impactful moments was a seminar on ethical AI that struck a chord with me.

The conversations I had after that seminar opened my eyes to the profound responsibility we bear as creators. I became determined to incorporate ethical considerations into my projects, advocating for a balanced approach that respects user privacy and fairness. This commitment has become a cornerstone of my work, shaping the AI systems I help develop.

The Joy of Mentorship

One of the most gratifying aspects of my journey has been the opportunity to mentor others in the realm of AI. Whether it's conducting workshops or providing guidance to budding professionals, I find immense fulfillment in sharing my knowledge.

Recently, I had the privilege of working with a group of enthusiastic graduate students on a project aimed at predicting energy consumption using AI. Their excitement and creativity were infectious. Watching them grapple with complex concepts and transform them into actionable insights was an exhilarating experience. It reaffirmed my belief that the future of AI lies in empowering the next generation of innovators.

Looking to the Horizon

As I reflect on my journey in artificial intelligence, I feel a sense of excitement about what lies ahead. The potential for AI to drive meaningful change across industries is boundless. I look forward to continuing my exploration of this field, seeking out new technologies and innovative solutions that can enhance human capabilities.

Through sharing these personal anecdotes, my hope is to inspire others to embrace the myriad opportunities that AI presents.

I genuinely welcome conversations about our collective experiences in this ever-evolving landscape, eager to learn from others and share my insights along the way.

Looking forward, I am committed to continually sharing my knowledge by publishing various content around this topic. Together, we can navigate the future of AI and unlock its full potential.

Welcome to a Journey Through HumIntel

In this book, we embark on an exciting exploration of the fascinating convergence between human intelligence and artificial intelligence—what I call **HumIntel**. From the dawn of intelligence in nature to the cutting-edge advancements in AI, we'll uncover how these two forms of intelligence intertwine to shape our present and future.

Each chapter delves into critical aspects of this evolving relationship. We'll start with the **foundations of human intelligence**, exploring what makes us unique, before transitioning to the **early developments in AI** and how these technologies have begun to augment our abilities. Along the way, we'll examine how AI adapts to our needs, learns alongside us, and enhances productivity through real-time tools.

In addition to practical insights, this journey will also highlight **global perspectives on AI adoption** and showcase successful collaborations between humans and machines across various industries. We'll touch on the ethical considerations of integrating AI into society and discuss the potential for a symbiotic relationship that maximizes human creativity and innovation.

As we navigate through these complex themes, expect to encounter **fun facts** that shed light on the incredible capabilities of AI, as well as a **touch of humor** to keep things light-hearted. After all, in the face of rapid technological change, it's essential to maintain our sense of wonder and joy.

So, let's dive in and discover the incredible possibilities that lie ahead as we merge human intuition with machine intelligence, paving the way for a brighter, more innovative future!

AI

Chapter 0

Genesis

The journey of intelligence begins with the earliest forms of life on Earth, where survival meant understanding the environment, making decisions, and adapting to changes. Even in the simplest organisms—like bacteria or insects—there are signs of intelligence. They navigate the world, find food, avoid dangers, and solve basic problems, all through instinctual processes that have been honed by evolution over millions of years.

For humans, intelligence has evolved into something far more complex. Our brains, made up of billions of neurons, allow us to not only survive but also thrive in diverse environments. We think deeply, imagine new ideas, solve complex problems, and communicate across cultures. It's this advanced intelligence that has enabled humans to build societies, develop technologies, and pursue creative endeavors like art and music. The human brain is a powerful organ, capable of learning, remembering, and feeling emotions—traits that have given us a unique place in the natural world.

But over the past century, a new kind of intelligence has been developing. For much of human history, the idea of machines that could think or act intelligently was confined to mythology or fiction. Ancient stories from around the world often imagined mechanical beings, but they were always the stuff of fantasy.

It wasn't until the 20th century, with the rise of modern computers, that these ideas began to take shape in reality. This shift—from intelligence existing only in living beings to the possibility of it being created in machines—marks a turning point in the history of intelligence.

Today, we see machines capable of processing vast amounts of information at incredible speeds. They can recognize patterns, solve problems, and even learn from their experiences. Unlike human intelligence, which evolved slowly over millennia, the intelligence in machines has progressed at an astonishing pace. It's not about imitating human thought—it's about using a different kind of processing power that can handle tasks we'd struggle to complete on our own. Machines have become tools that help us analyze data, make predictions, and improve efficiency in ways we never imagined.

The integration of technology with human knowledge has opened new doors. In medicine, machines assist doctors in diagnosing illnesses by analyzing data that would take a human years to sift through.

Yet, this raises important questions. What does it mean to be intelligent? How do we define the boundaries of intelligence when it no longer applies only to living creatures? As technology continues to evolve, these questions become more pressing. The distinction between natural and artificial intelligence blurs as both humans and machines find new ways to interact and grow.

Machines could provide insights by processing vast quantities of information, allowing us to see connections we might otherwise miss. This isn't just about machines doing things for us; it's about them helping us achieve more than we ever could on our own.

We can already see hints of this collaboration in everyday life. Tools that personalize education to fit a student's needs make learning more accessible and effective. In the workplace, automation frees up time for creative and strategic thinking, allowing people to focus on what they do best. The possibilities are endless, and the more we embrace this partnership, the more potential we unlock.

At the same time, this rapid progress comes with challenges. How do we ensure that technology is used responsibly? How do we maintain control over systems that are becoming increasingly complex? There are ethical concerns that we need to address, especially as machines become more capable of decision-making. It's vital to create safeguards that ensure these tools benefit humanity and do not lead to unintended consequences.

The evolving relationship between human knowledge and technology isn't about competition, but rather cooperation. Humans will always bring unique qualities to the table—imagination, moral reasoning, and emotional understanding. Machines, on the other hand, bring speed, accuracy, and the ability to process information in ways that are simply beyond human capabilities. Together, they have the potential to create something far greater than either could achieve alone.

As we look to the future, it's clear that the growth of technology is not the end of human intelligence—it's a new chapter. The story of intelligence began with the earliest life forms and has now expanded into realms we once thought were unattainable. The journey continues, and as humans and machines continue to learn from and grow with one another, the possibilities for discovery, creativity, and progress are limitless.

This shift also compels us to confront a future where our relationship with knowledge itself may transform. If intelligence becomes something we share with machines, does that redefine the essence of being human? Does it amplify our potential, or risk diluting the qualities that make us uniquely human? These are not just philosophical musings but essential questions for our time. In the dance of co-evolution between humans and machines, the choreography remains unwritten—offering both promise and uncertainty. For every door technology opens, there is a mirror held up to humanity, asking us to reflect on who we are and who we aspire to become.

Real-Life Example: Evolutionary Intelligence in Bees and AI in Autonomous Vehicles

In nature, bees display remarkable problem-solving skills. They can navigate long distances, communicate with other bees about the location of food, and solve complex challenges, like optimizing their routes to minimize energy expenditure. This is an example of biological intelligence at work, where cognitive ability evolves to increase survival chances.

On the other hand, artificial intelligence has shown similar feats in areas like autonomous driving. Companies such as **Tesla** and **Waymo** have developed AI-powered autonomous vehicles capable of navigating complex environments without human intervention. These vehicles process vast amounts of sensory data (cameras, radar, lidar) to identify objects, predict behavior, and make real-time decisions, much like how bees interpret environmental cues to find food sources. The AI in autonomous cars replicates a kind of navigation intelligence, but it's the product of human design, rather than evolutionary biology.

Analogy

Think of AI like learning to ride a bike. At first, you're wobbly and need training wheels. Over time, you get better, and soon, you're zooming ahead of your friends. AI is the same—it started slow but is now learning faster than ever before

Why It Matters: The comparison of bees' evolutionary intelligence and AI in autonomous vehicles highlights how nature inspires technology. Bees' navigation and problem-solving skills inform AI systems like autonomous driving, emphasizing resource efficiency and adaptability. This cross-disciplinary learning fosters innovations that enhance sustainability and collaboration. Understanding biological intelligence refines AI design, mirroring nature's efficiency. Both systems optimize resources, offering models for sustainable solutions. Ultimately, this synergy reshapes industries and expands human capabilities.

Reference: Autonomous Vehicle AI - Waymo

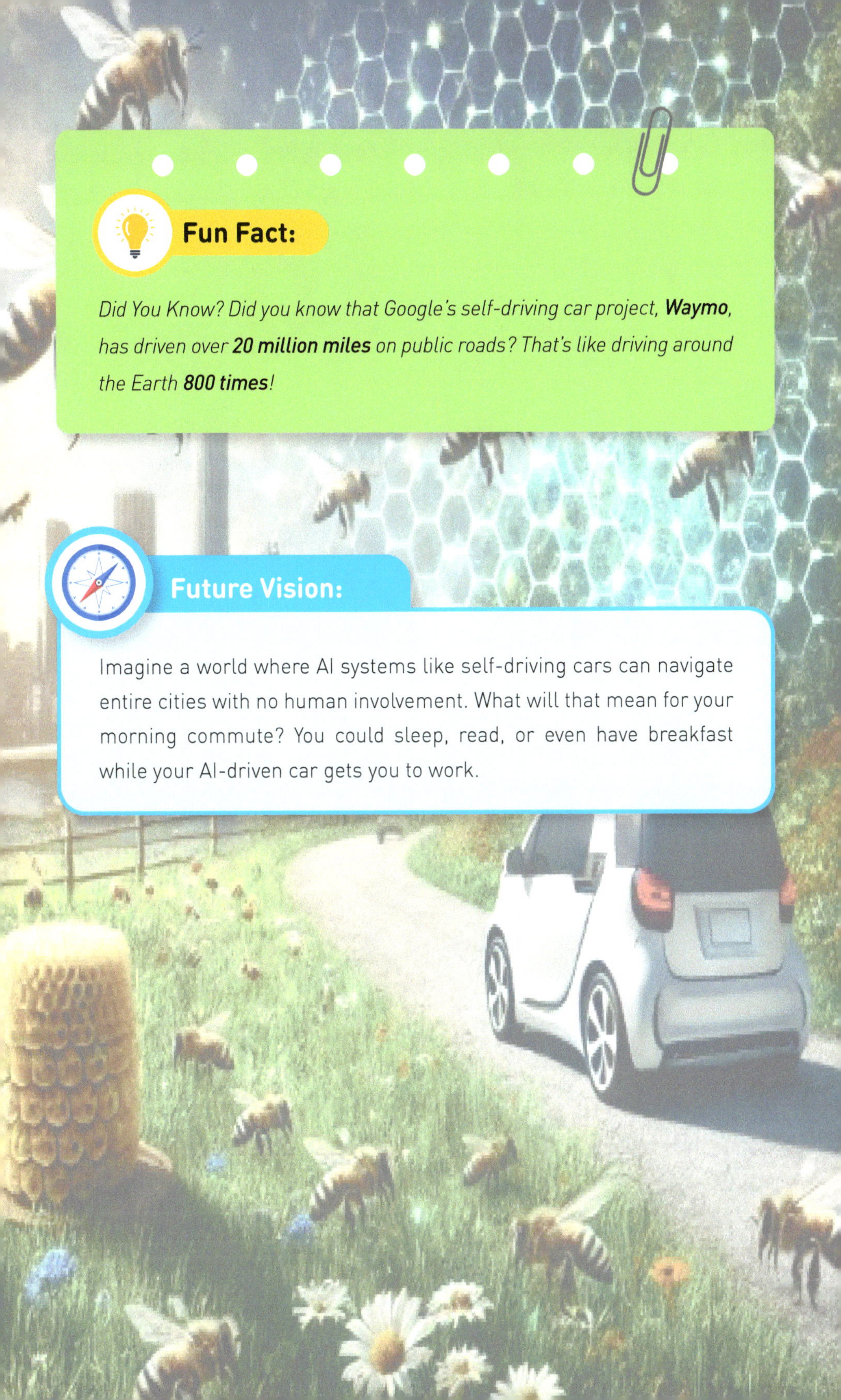

Fun Fact:

*Did You Know? Did you know that Google's self-driving car project, **Waymo**, has driven over **20 million miles** on public roads? That's like driving around the Earth **800 times**!*

Future Vision:

Imagine a world where AI systems like self-driving cars can navigate entire cities with no human involvement. What will that mean for your morning commute? You could sleep, read, or even have breakfast while your AI-driven car gets you to work.

0.2   Defining the roots of human intelligence

Human intelligence has its roots in survival. Millions of years ago, early humans used their intelligence for basic tasks: finding food, avoiding predators, and building shelter. This practical, trial-and-error-based problem-solving was essential for survival. Over time, this evolved into more complex forms of intelligence. Humans developed the ability to think abstractly, plan for the future, and reflect on their environment, which set them apart from other animals.

The human brain, with its billions of neurons, plays a critical role in this cognitive evolution. These neurons form intricate networks that process information, allowing humans to learn from experiences and adapt to new situations. As intelligence grew, language emerged as one of the most significant milestones. While many animals communicate, humans created structured language, enabling the sharing of complex ideas and emotions. This allowed for collaboration, leading to the development of societies and cultures. Language also enabled the transfer of knowledge across generations, ensuring progress through collective learning.

This "collective intelligence" is one of the defining features of human evolution. Unlike animals that rely on instinct, humans can build on each other's experiences, solving problems faster and innovating more rapidly. This collective intelligence is the reason behind major advancements, such as agriculture, city-building, and technology. Human intelligence is not limited to logic and problem-solving, though. Creativity plays a vital role. Humans imagine things that don't yet exist and bring them into reality, driving innovation in fields such as art, science, and literature.

Social interaction is another key aspect of human intelligence. Humans are inherently social beings, and their relationships shape much of their cognitive development. The ability to understand, empathize, and collaborate with others is crucial in building societies and achieving common goals. This social intelligence has helped humans thrive in both small groups and large, complex cities.

Over time, human intelligence has become more advanced, giving rise to fields like science, philosophy, and the arts. These represent the pinnacle of thousands of years of cognitive evolution, built on the shared knowledge of generations. Science, in particular, has unlocked the mysteries of the universe, from the smallest particles to the largest galaxies.

In the last century, technology has introduced a new chapter in human intelligence. Machines, especially computers, assist in performing tasks previously unimaginable, such as processing vast amounts of data. Artificial intelligence (AI) represents the next frontier, with the potential to revolutionize the way we live and work. However, it also raises questions: How does AI differ from human intelligence, and how can humans use AI to enhance, rather than replace, their cognitive abilities?

Human intelligence will continue to evolve, shaped by new technologies and ways of thinking. The integration of human and artificial intelligence holds great potential for future advancements in science and medicine. However, it's vital to approach this evolution carefully, ensuring that technology is used to enhance human life rather than diminish it.

At its heart, human intelligence is more than a set of abilities—it's a story. A story of survival, yes, but also one of endless curiosity and boundless imagination. It's what allows us to ask the big questions: *Why are we here? What's beyond the stars? What's next?*. This constant drive to learn, adapt, and create is what has propelled us from the savannas to skyscrapers, from cave paintings to quantum theories. It's a journey that feels uniquely human—a restless, beautiful search for meaning in the chaos of existence.

But here's the fascinating part: human intelligence isn't static. It's fluid, evolving, growing, and reshaping itself with every challenge we face and every breakthrough we achieve. Just as our ancestors forged tools to survive, we now build technologies that push the limits of what we can imagine. As we stand on the brink of merging our intelligence with artificial systems, the lines between creator and collaborator blur. It's not just about how intelligence has brought us here—it's about where it will take us next.

Real-Life Example: Human Collaboration and Language in Google's Knowledge Graph

Human intelligence is unique due to our ability to communicate and collaborate. This collaborative nature has reached unprecedented levels in the digital age. A prime example is **Google's Knowledge Graph**, a system that collects and organizes information from around the world. By processing millions of data points, the Knowledge Graph allows users to search for anything and receive highly relevant, curated information.

This concept builds on centuries of human collaboration and communication, dating back to the development of written language and shared knowledge systems, such as libraries and encyclopedias. Google's tool is an extension of human intelligence, allowing individuals to tap into a vast collective memory far beyond what any one person could retain.

Why It Matters: Google's Knowledge Graph exemplifies how digital tools extend human intelligence by amplifying collaboration and communication. It transforms centuries of shared knowledge into an accessible, dynamic resource, empowering individuals to make informed decisions and innovate faster than ever before. This synergy of human ingenuity and AI drives progress on a global scale.

Reference: Google's Knowledge Graph

Analogy

Imagine the human brain as a library, where each book represents a memory or a skill. Some people have bigger libraries than others, but what makes human intelligence so powerful is that we can share our "books" with others. The internet, especially Google, has become the world's largest library, where everyone contributes to the shelves.

Fun Fact

*Did you know the human brain has about **86 billion neurons**? That's almost as many stars as there are in the Milky Way galaxy!*

Interactive Thought

Try this: Next time you're with a group of friends, each person should describe what comes to mind when they hear the word "apple." One might think of the fruit, another might think of the company, and someone else might think of the story of Adam and Eve. Now imagine an AI trying to do the same thing—it would need a Knowledge Graph like Google's to understand all the meanings.

Future Vision:

Imagine a future where the Knowledge Graph becomes so advanced that it can create personalized learning experiences. It could guide you through learning a new language or mastering a musical instrument, anticipating your needs like a tutor who knows exactly what you're ready to learn next.

0.3 Birth of AI: early developments and conceptual frameworks

Artificial intelligence (AI) has its roots in an old human curiosity: understanding and recreating intelligence. For centuries, people imagined creating machines with human-like minds. But it wasn't until the mid-20th century that AI became a real field of study. Scientists started seriously exploring how to make machines think like humans.

One of the most important figures in this early period was Alan Turing, a brilliant mathematician. In the 1930s and 1940s, Turing introduced some groundbreaking ideas that changed how we think about machine intelligence. He believed that if you could program machines to follow instructions, they could solve problems, just like humans. This idea was revolutionary and laid the foundation for the first computers and AI.

In 1950, Turing came up with the famous "Turing Test." He suggested that if a machine could have a conversation with a person and make them think they were talking to another human, that machine could be called "intelligent." This was a huge turning point because it made people question whether intelligence was something only humans could have.

A few years later, in 1956, AI officially became a field of study at a conference held at Dartmouth College. Leading scientists like John McCarthy and Marvin Minsky gathered to discuss how machines could mimic human thinking and learning. McCarthy also coined the term "artificial intelligence" at this conference, and it became the starting point for building intelligent machines.

At first, AI research focused on getting machines to do specific tasks, like solving math problems or playing games. These early programs followed strict rules, so they could only work on a limited set of tasks. While these programs were impressive at first, they were not very adaptable. They couldn't think creatively or handle new situations the way humans do.

As researchers continued, they realized that true intelligence needed more than just following rules. This led to the rise of machine learning in the 1980s. Instead of telling machines exactly what to do, machine learning allowed systems to learn from data, adjust their behavior, and improve over time. This was a big shift because now, AI could learn on its own through experience.

Another important development during this time was neural networks, inspired by the way the human brain works. Neural networks allowed machines to process information more like humans. While early versions were simple, they showed a lot of promise for making machines smarter and more flexible.

Despite these breakthroughs, progress in AI was slow for a long time. Researchers faced challenges like processing huge amounts of data and getting machines to understand real-world situations. AI went through phases of high hopes and disappointing results. But things changed in the 1990s and 2000s, thanks to better technology, faster computers, and more access to large amounts of data. The rise of the internet and more powerful processors helped AI take big steps forward.

A major breakthrough was deep learning, which uses multi-layered neural networks to handle large amounts of data. Deep learning allowed AI to take on more complex tasks, such as recognizing images, understanding natural language, and even creating new content.

Today, AI is more powerful and useful than ever before. It's being used in many areas, like healthcare, finance, and even entertainment. AI helps doctors diagnose diseases, assists companies in making financial decisions, and improves how we interact with technology, like personalized recommendations online. What makes modern AI so powerful is its ability to keep learning and improving by analyzing huge amounts of data.

However, as AI becomes more advanced, it raises some important questions about its impact on society. AI has the potential to solve many big problems, but it also brings concerns like privacy and fairness. How we develop and use AI in the future will shape its role in the world, and it's important to ensure it benefits humanity while being transparent and ethical.

As we look at the path AI has taken, it's fascinating to think about how far we've come and what's still ahead. What will the next wave of AI innovation look like? Will machines truly become self-aware one day, as science fiction often suggests? While the technological advances have been remarkable, the philosophical questions persist. As AI continues to evolve, should we be worried about the ethical implications of machines making decisions that impact our lives? And how do we ensure that the creators of these intelligent systems remain responsible for the outcomes?

Moreover, as we see AI making strides in almost every sector, it's worth asking: what happens when machines begin to surpass human abilities in certain tasks? Will we embrace AI as an extension of our own creativity and intelligence, or will it become a source of tension and competition? Will this spark a revolution in creativity, or will it prompt a backlash against technology's role in our most human endeavors? Only time will tell, but one thing is certain: the journey of AI has just begun, and its impact on our world will continue to unfold in ways we can't fully predict.

In summary, AI's birth and growth have transformed it from a theoretical idea into something that's changing how we live and work. The journey of AI, from its early beginnings to today's advanced systems, shows both its huge potential and the challenges we still need to figure out.

Real-Life Example: IBM's Deep Blue and AlphaGo

The birth of artificial intelligence was marked by machines performing tasks that were once thought to require human thought. One early milestone was **IBM's Deep Blue**, which defeated world chess champion Garry Kasparov in 1997. This was a big deal because chess was seen as the ultimate test of strategy and intelligence. More recently, **AlphaGo**, an AI created by Google's DeepMind, took this to the next level by defeating a world champion at the game of Go, which is far more complex than chess.

Why It Matters: IBM's Deep Blue and AlphaGo show how AI can surpass human limitations in complex tasks once thought exclusive to human intelligence. These breakthroughs not only challenge our understanding of intelligence but also demonstrate AI's potential to solve problems beyond human capability. They highlight the transformative impact AI can have on fields requiring strategy, creativity, and deep thinking.

Reference: AlphaGo – DeepMind

Storytelling:

In the mid-90s, people couldn't believe a computer could defeat a chess champion. Deep Blue wasn't a genius like Kasparov—it was a brute force machine, analyzing millions of moves per second. But in 2016, AlphaGo shocked the world by beating a Go champion. It didn't just calculate moves—it learned strategies from millions of games. It was as if AlphaGo was learning to "think" about the game in ways even humans couldn't predict.

Humor:

If Deep Blue and AlphaGo were kids in school, Deep Blue would be the kid who memorized every book in the library, while AlphaGo would be the genius who learns a new way to do math that even the teacher hadn't thought of.

Fun Fact:

Did you know that in 1997, when Deep Blue defeated Kasparov, it could evaluate **200 million chess positions per second***? That's like thinking through every possible move in a game of chess faster than you can blink!*

Future Vision:

Picture yourself sitting in a creative meeting. Instead of being an observer, AI serves as an active participant, offering innovative ideas and insights. With its vast database of knowledge and predictive capabilities, AI can brainstorm alongside you, suggesting solutions that blend human creativity with machine precision.

0.4   The intersection of human and machine: laying the foundation for HumIntel

HumIntel is an exciting idea about how humans and machines can collaborate in the future. Instead of seeing human intelligence and artificial intelligence (AI) as competitors, HumIntel envisions a partnership where both can enhance each other. This isn't about who's better; it's about combining our unique strengths to create something amazing.

Humans have a special way of understanding the world. We use creativity, intuition, and emotional intelligence to solve problems. Our thinking goes beyond just logic—we draw on feelings and experiences, allowing us to think outside the box. This gives us a kind of intelligence that machines, despite their speed and efficiency, don't have. On the flip side, machines are great at quickly processing large amounts of data and handling repetitive tasks without making mistakes. They can spot patterns in ways humans can't manage alone. The goal of HumIntel is to merge these strengths for a new kind of teamwork.

At its core, HumIntel recognizes that humans and machines can complement each other in ways that open up new opportunities. Machines can help us sort through complex information, but humans add context, creativity, and judgment to make that information meaningful. For instance, in healthcare, AI can analyze patient data and identify trends, but a doctor's experience and gut feeling are crucial for interpreting those results and making the final call. While machines assist, humans remain central to decision-making, adding layers of understanding that machines can't reach.

Creativity is another area where HumIntel shines. While AI can generate ideas and analyze trends, it's the human touch that gives depth and emotional connection to creative work. Machines can produce ideas and mimic some creative processes, but humans bring imagination, emotions, and cultural insights that make creations truly impactful. When AI and human creativity come together, the results are richer and more meaningful.

This partnership isn't just limited to fields like medicine or art; HumIntel influences our everyday lives. As AI becomes more common, from digital assistants to recommendation systems, the importance of human judgment becomes clear. While machines can offer suggestions, humans are still needed to decide how to act. Machines provide data, but it's humans who interpret and apply it based on ethical, emotional, and cultural values. The future of AI is not about machines replacing humans, but about both working together to achieve more than either could on their own.

HumIntel also acknowledges the limitations of both human and machine intelligence. Machines excel in precision and efficiency but lack the subtlety and depth of human understanding. Conversely, human intelligence is rich in context and creativity but struggles with processing vast amounts of information. By combining the two, we can create a fuller form of intelligence that harnesses both strengths.

The education sector stands to gain a lot from HumIntel as well. AI can personalize learning by analyzing students' needs and adapting lessons to suit them. However, it's the human aspect—the teachers, mentors, and classmates—that truly enrich the learning experience. Machines can provide resources, but humans offer encouragement, guidance, and a sense of community that technology can't replace. The future of education lies in blending machine efficiency with human connection to foster deeper, more personalized learning experiences.

As AI continues to grow, it's evident that humans play a vital role in ensuring these technologies are used ethically. Machines, no matter how smart, don't have a moral compass. They can be programmed to follow ethical rules, but only humans can navigate the complex ethical dilemmas of the real world. Humans bring empathy and fairness to the table, ensuring AI benefits society as a whole instead of creating or worsening inequalities. HumIntel emphasizes the need for human oversight to make sure AI advances in ethical and inclusive ways.

Looking ahead, HumIntel offers a way forward that highlights collaboration between humans and machines. It's about working together to achieve goals that neither could accomplish alone. This partnership can transform industries, drive innovation, and enhance our everyday lives.

HumIntel also envisions a future where machines empower humans to reach new heights of creativity and innovation. By taking care of repetitive, data-heavy tasks, AI frees people to focus on more creative and strategic work. This can lead to a more fulfilling work environment where human workers aren't weighed down by mundane tasks but are inspired to explore new ideas and push boundaries. The result is a more engaged workforce, where the partnership between humans and machines unlocks incredible possibilities.

As we look to the future, HumIntel serves as a blueprint for a new kind of intelligence. It's a vision where human creativity, emotional depth, and ethical understanding work hand in hand with the processing power and efficiency of machines. This collaboration between humans and AI will shape how we live, work, and interact with the world. By recognizing both strengths and limitations, we can create a future where humans and machines enhance each other's abilities, paving the way for innovation, progress, and understanding.

In this future, the relationship between humans and machines is one of partnership, not replacement. It's about finding a balance where both can thrive and improve each other. HumIntel represents a shift in how we view intelligence—not as something that belongs only to humans or machines, but as something that can be shared and elevated through collaboration. This is the future of intelligence, where human creativity and emotional insight meet the computational power of machines, opening up exciting new possibilities for what we can achieve together.

Real-Life Example: AI in Medical Diagnosis

The merging of human and machine intelligence is already happening in healthcare. For instance, **IBM's Watson** can analyze medical data to help doctors diagnose illnesses, particularly in detecting early signs of cancer. While Watson can look at thousands of studies and patient histories in minutes, it doesn't replace doctors. Instead, it works with them to make better decisions, faster. The doctor still brings emotional intelligence and understanding of the patient, which AI cannot replicate.

Why It Matters: The integration of AI in medical diagnosis demonstrates the potential of human-AI collaboration to enhance healthcare outcomes. By enabling faster, more accurate diagnoses, AI can help doctors save lives and improve treatment plans, benefiting patients globally. This progress underscores the importance of leveraging technology to address complex challenges and improve access to high-quality care for all.

Reference: IBM Watson Health - AI in Medical Diagnosis

Analogy

Think of the relationship between AI and doctors like Batman and his gadgets. Batman is already a great detective, but his tools, like his supercomputer, help him solve crimes even faster. Similarly, AI is the ultimate tool, enhancing what humans can already do.

Storytelling:

Imagine going to the doctor and instead of a long wait for test results, AI-powered systems quickly scan your data, compare it to thousands of similar cases, and instantly offer insights. It's not replacing your doctor; it's giving your doctor a superpower to make sure no detail is overlooked.

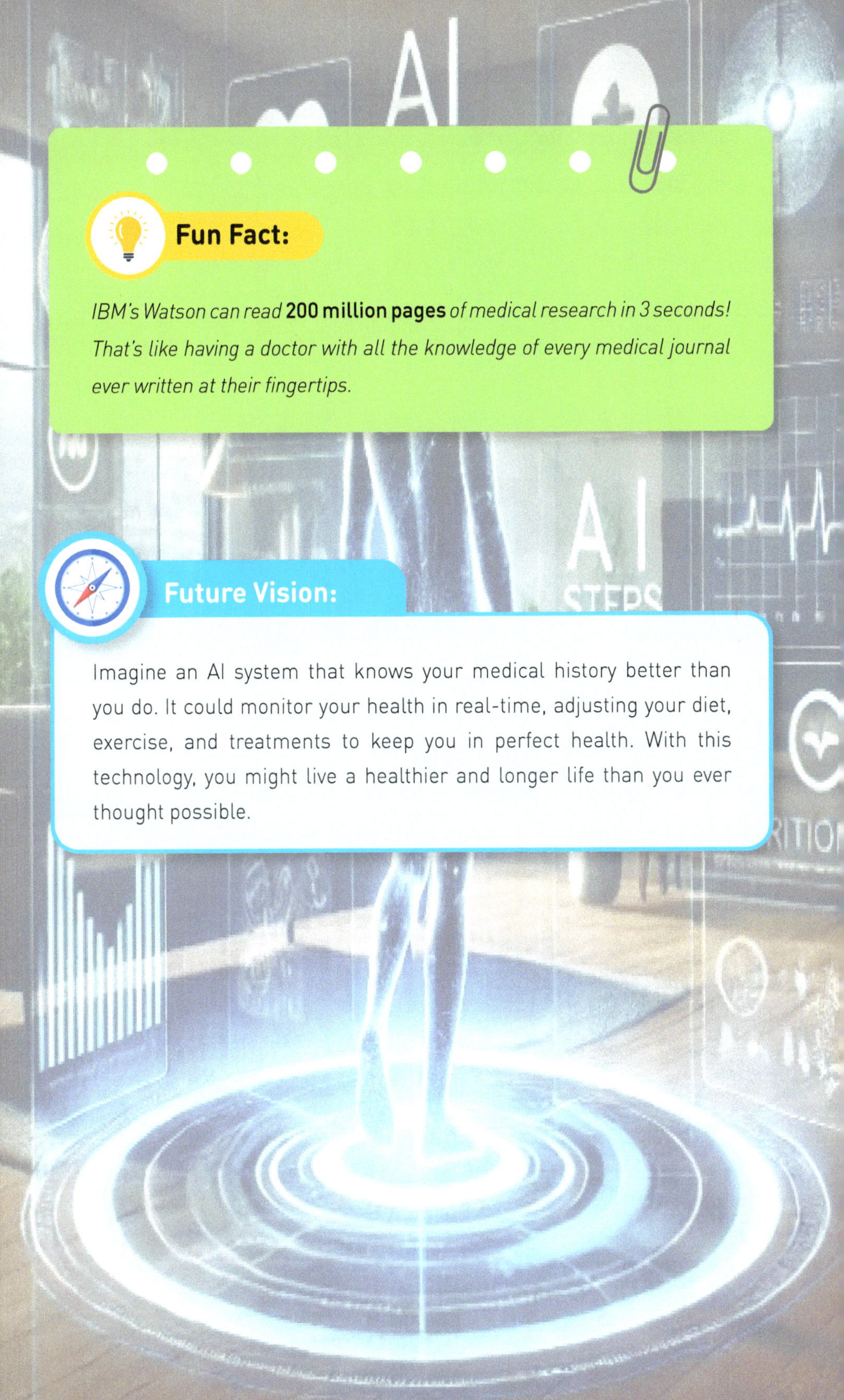

Fun Fact:

IBM's Watson can read **200 million pages** of medical research in 3 seconds! That's like having a doctor with all the knowledge of every medical journal ever written at their fingertips.

Future Vision:

Imagine an AI system that knows your medical history better than you do. It could monitor your health in real-time, adjusting your diet, exercise, and treatments to keep you in perfect health. With this technology, you might live a healthier and longer life than you ever thought possible.

0.5 The quest for augmentation: moving beyond natural limits

Human intelligence has always been about growth and discovery. We know our thinking abilities are impressive, but we also understand they have limits. For example, we can only handle a certain amount of information at one time, and sometimes our emotions can get in the way of good decision-making. Things like biases and short attention spans can make it hard to think clearly and can hold us back.

Looking back at history, it's clear that humans have always tried to go beyond these limitations. From the beginning, people have created tools to improve both their physical and mental abilities. For instance, the wheel was not just a simple invention; it changed how we move and transport things. The invention of written language helped us communicate better and share knowledge for future generations. Later, innovations like the printing press and the internet made it easier to connect with others and access a huge amount of information. Each of these developments shows our ongoing desire to improve and overcome our natural constraints.

Today, artificial intelligence (AI) is leading this quest for enhancement. AI has the potential to boost our thinking abilities and change how we approach complex tasks and decisions. With AI in our daily lives, we can analyze huge amounts of data quickly and accurately, helping us make better choices and focus on deeper thinking.

However, AI's impact goes beyond just making things easier. It encourages us to rethink what intelligence means. Instead of seeing AI as a replacement for human thought, we can view it as a helpful tool that enhances our abilities and inspires new ways of thinking. This teamwork between humans and machines broadens our understanding of intelligence, highlighting the unique strengths of both.

As we integrate AI into our lives, we must recognize how it can improve our creativity and problem-solving skills. AI can analyze complex data, identify patterns, and generate insights that we might miss. This ability allows us to tackle challenges from new angles, leading to innovative solutions and fresh ideas.

The relationship between human intelligence and AI is a partnership where both can learn from each other. Humans bring creativity, intuition, and emotional understanding, while AI offers analytical power and the ability to handle vast amounts of information. Together, this collaboration can spark new ideas and breakthroughs that neither humans nor machines could achieve alone.

To fully benefit from this partnership, we need to embrace collaboration between humans and machines. It's not just about using technology; it's about rethinking how we learn, innovate, and express creativity. By leveraging AI's strengths, we can enhance our problem-solving skills and create a culture of curiosity and exploration.

This journey isn't without challenges. As we bring AI into our lives, we must be aware of the ethical implications of these advancements. It's essential to ensure that AI aligns with our values and that we prioritize fairness, transparency, and accountability.

What happens when AI goes beyond merely assisting human intelligence and starts actively enhancing it? Could machines unlock untapped areas of human creativity, pushing us into realms of innovation we never thought possible? The growing integration of AI into fields like medicine, design, and even social change is pushing us to rethink what it means to be truly human. As this journey of augmentation continues, we are left to wonder about the fine balance between progress and preservation of what makes us human.

In summary, the quest for improvement is a shared journey of discovery and growth. The partnership between human and machine intelligence has the potential to shape our future significantly. By nurturing this collaboration, we can open up new opportunities for creativity, innovation, and progress, enriching our intelligence and expanding our understanding of what is possible.

Real-Life Example: AI-Assisted Creativity in Art and Music

AI is not just for logical tasks like diagnosing diseases or driving cars—it's also pushing the boundaries of human creativity. **AIVA**, an AI music composer, has created original music used in video games and films. The music it creates is based on patterns it's learned from analyzing thousands of pieces of classical music. But while AI can write the notes, human musicians often refine the compositions, adding emotion and nuance.

Similarly, AI-generated art is becoming popular. A portrait created by AI called **Edmond de Belamy** was auctioned for over $400,000. However, the AI didn't work alone—human artists selected and curated the pieces.

Why It Matters: The integration of AI into creative fields is reshaping our understanding of artistic expression. By learning from vast datasets, AI systems can produce works of music, visual art, and literature that exhibit complexity and originality, bridging the gap between technology and human creativity. This collaboration expands the possibilities of what is considered art and opens new avenues for innovation in creative industries.

Analogy

Imagine AI as a junior chef in the kitchen. It follows recipes perfectly but doesn't know how to experiment with flavors or make adjustments for taste. A master chef, however, can use the junior chef to handle the basics while they focus on adding that creative flair.

Reference:

- AIVA - AI Music Composer
- Christie's - AI-Generated Art Auction

Humor:

If AI and humans worked together to create a song, AI would be like the drummer who keeps perfect rhythm but doesn't write the lyrics, while the human would be the lead singer pouring out emotion into every note.

Fun Fact:

Did you know that AI has already co-written pop songs? In 2016, an AI system helped create the song "Daddy's Car," which sounds like a Beatles track.

Future Vision:

In the future, AI might become a co-creator in everything. Imagine being able to describe a story idea, and AI creates the first draft, leaving you to refine the characters and plot. The combination of human creativity and AI's vast knowledge could lead to a new golden age of entertainment and art.

Chapter 1

Evolution of HumIntel

In an age where technology is rapidly evolving, the concept of HumIntel emerges as a pivotal bridge between two distinct yet complementary forms of intelligence—human and artificial. The term itself, a fusion of "human" and "intelligence," signifies not just the coexistence of these two entities but also their potential to enhance one another in profound ways. By acknowledging and embracing the unique capabilities of both, we open the door to a future rich in innovation and collaboration.

At its core, HumIntel highlights the intrinsic strengths that each form of intelligence brings to the table. Humans are inherently creative beings, equipped with the capacity for abstract thought and emotional intelligence. Our ability to create, innovate, and empathize sets us apart from machines. We draw on our experiences, cultural backgrounds, and social connections to navigate the complexities of life. Whether it's crafting a compelling story, devising a groundbreaking solution to a problem, or simply understanding a friend's emotions, our intelligence is deeply rooted in our humanity.

In contrast, artificial intelligence thrives on data. Machines are capable of processing vast amounts of information at lightning speed, performing intricate calculations, and identifying patterns that often elude human perception. AI's strength lies in its ability to analyze and synthesize data, drawing insights that can inform decisions, streamline processes, and enhance productivity. However, despite these remarkable capabilities, AI lacks the nuanced understanding of context and the ethical considerations that only humans can provide.

The magic of HumIntel lies in the synergy created when these two intelligences collaborate. Imagine a world where AI is not viewed as a rival to human capability but as a powerful ally. In such a world, machines would handle the heavy lifting of data analysis while humans inject creativity, context, and ethical reasoning into the decision-making process. This partnership has the potential to unlock solutions to challenges that, until now, have seemed insurmountable.

Consider the transformative possibilities that arise when human creativity meets AI's analytical power. In the fields of science and medicine, for instance, AI can assist researchers in analyzing complex data sets, identifying potential breakthroughs, and accelerating the pace of discovery. Yet, it is the human researchers who bring context to those findings, using their insights to guide the direction of research and ensure that the outcomes serve the greater good. Together, they create a powerful alliance that drives innovation and advances our understanding of the world.

Moreover, HumIntel paves the way for a more ethical approach to technology. By integrating human judgment into AI decision-making processes, we can ensure that the values and ethics of society are upheld. This is particularly critical in areas such as criminal justice, healthcare, and finance, where decisions made by AI can have significant consequences for individuals and communities. Humans must remain at the forefront of these conversations, advocating for fairness, accountability, and transparency in the deployment of AI technologies.

As we navigate the complexities of a rapidly changing world, the partnership between human intelligence and AI becomes increasingly vital. The challenges we face today—climate change, public health crises, and social inequalities—require innovative solutions that harness the strengths of both forms of intelligence. By fostering collaboration between humans and machines, we can develop strategies that are not only effective but also compassionate and considerate of the diverse perspectives that shape our world.

To fully realize the potential of HumIntel, we must also prioritize education and training that equips individuals with the skills necessary to thrive in a technology-driven landscape. This includes fostering digital literacy, critical thinking, and emotional intelligence. As the nature of work evolves, individuals must learn how to leverage AI tools while retaining their unique contributions. This involves understanding how to collaborate with AI, using its capabilities to enhance creativity and problem-solving rather than viewing it as a threat to employment.

In this new paradigm, creativity will flourish alongside technology. Artists, writers, musicians, and creators can harness AI as a collaborator, generating ideas and exploring new avenues of expression. By blending human intuition and emotion with AI's analytical prowess, we can push the boundaries of creativity, producing works that resonate on deeper levels and challenge the status quo. This collaborative approach can lead to a renaissance of innovation, where the fusion of human and artificial intelligence results in art, literature, and technology that inspires and captivates.

However, as we embrace the promise of HumIntel, we must remain vigilant about the ethical implications of AI development. Discussions surrounding privacy, bias, and the societal impact of AI technologies must be ongoing and inclusive. Stakeholders from various sectors—technologists, ethicists, policymakers, and the public—should engage in conversations that shape the future of AI and ensure that it aligns with the collective good. By fostering a culture of accountability and transparency, we can navigate the challenges presented by AI and create a future where technology serves humanity.

In conclusion, HumIntel embodies a transformative vision for the future—one where human creativity and artificial intelligence work in tandem to elevate our capabilities and address the complex challenges of our time. This partnership holds the potential to drive innovation, enhance decision-making, and reshape entire industries. By recognizing and celebrating the unique strengths of both human and artificial intelligence, we can forge a path toward a more compassionate, ethical, and innovative world. The journey ahead invites us to embrace the possibilities that lie at the intersection of these two forms of intelligence, ultimately enriching our lives and empowering us to create a better tomorrow..

Real-Life Example: A real-world example of this synthesis is AI-powered drug discovery

AI is transforming drug discovery, with companies like Atomwise leading the charge. By analyzing millions of chemical compounds, AI systems identify potential candidates for new medications, a process that once took years. This innovation significantly shortens development timelines, allowing treatments to reach patients faster. AI takes on the heavy lifting of data analysis, uncovering patterns and possibilities at an unprecedented scale, while human researchers concentrate on interpreting the findings, designing experiments, and navigating the ethical complexities of clinical trials. Together, they achieve outcomes neither could accomplish alone, showcasing the power of human-AI collaboration in healthcare innovation.

Why It Matters: The impact of AI in drug discovery is revolutionizing the healthcare industry, accelerating the path from research to treatment in ways that were once unimaginable. AI's ability to process and analyze vast amounts of data quickly is dramatically reducing the time needed to identify promising drug candidates. But it's not just about speed—it's about precision.

Reference:

- Atomwise: (https://www.atomwise.com)

- "AI and Machine Learning in Drug Discovery," *Nature Biotechnology* (2018) (https://www.nature.com/articles/nbt.4291)

Analogy

Imagine crafting a masterpiece painting. AI acts as the diligent apprentice, preparing the canvas, mixing the perfect shades of paint, and laying down the base strokes with precision. The human artist then steps in to add depth, emotion, and nuance, transforming the work into an inspiring creation. This seamless teamwork ensures both speed and artistry in achieving a remarkable result.

Fun Fact

AI can analyze and compare over 100,000 chemical compounds in less time than it takes for a human to brew a cup of coffee. Yet, it still depends on human researchers to turn those discoveries into life-saving medications.

Humor:

Imagine AI trying to come up with a cure for the common cold and saying, "I've processed 10 million data points, but humans still haven't figured out why they keep shaking hands at parties."

Future Vision:

As HumIntel continues to evolve, we might see a future where AI assists humans in tackling more abstract challenges like philosophy or ethics. Imagine an AI that helps people make personal life decisions—like career choices or relationships—based on analyzing vast amounts of psychological and social data. This AI-human collaboration could reshape not just industries but the very way we live our lives.

1.2 Tracing the Growth of Cognitive Technologies in Human History

The evolution of cognitive technologies is an extraordinary narrative that captures humanity's relentless drive to enhance mental capabilities. This journey spans countless generations, starting with rudimentary tools and advancing to the advanced systems we depend on today. As we explore this rich history, we uncover the profound impact cognitive technologies have had on shaping our societies, influencing our thought processes, learning methods, and the way we engage with the world around us.

Our story begins long ago, in a time when early humans faced the challenge of managing information with limited cognitive tools. Simple instruments like tally sticks and stones emerged as our ancestors sought ways to aid their memory and improve their ability to manipulate information. These initial tools were not merely extensions of our minds; they represented humanity's first steps toward overcoming natural cognitive limits. They laid the groundwork for a future where the synergy between humans and their tools would redefine intellectual performance.

One of the earliest significant advancements in cognitive technology was the invention of the abacus. This ancient counting device allowed users to perform arithmetic calculations with greater accuracy and efficiency. By providing a tactile method for representing numbers, the abacus transformed mathematical thinking, enabling early civilizations to manage trade, resources, and societal organization more effectively. It was not merely a calculating tool; it fostered a deeper understanding of numerical relationships and paved the way for more complex mathematical concepts.

As societies progressed, so too did the tools designed to help humans manage and process information. The mechanical clock, which emerged during the Middle Ages, marked another revolutionary leap forward. This invention fundamentally altered how people perceived and organized time. By introducing a precise method for tracking hours and minutes, the clock allowed for a more structured approach to daily life. Communities began to synchronize their activities, enhancing productivity and establishing the rhythms of work and rest. The impact of the mechanical clock extended beyond timekeeping; it influenced social structures, economic systems, and even cultural practices, as people increasingly organized their lives around the predictable patterns dictated by time.

With the dawn of the printing press in the 15th century, the landscape of knowledge dissemination changed dramatically. This groundbreaking invention mechanized the production of written material, allowing texts to be reproduced in large quantities. As a result, access to information became more widespread, democratizing knowledge and fostering literacy on an unprecedented scale. The printing press empowered individuals to share ideas, challenge prevailing narratives, and engage in intellectual discourse. This shift not only transformed the flow of information but also nurtured a culture of inquiry that would fuel the Renaissance and Enlightenment, shaping modern thought.

The 20th century ushered in a technological revolution that further accelerated the growth of cognitive technologies. The invention of the personal computer heralded a new era in human-computer interaction. For the first time, powerful computing capabilities became accessible to individuals, allowing them to perform complex tasks, manage vast amounts of data, and create content with relative ease. The personal computer revolutionized the way people engaged with information, enabling creativity and innovation to flourish. It became a powerful tool for self-expression, collaboration, and exploration, transforming not only individual lives but also entire industries.

The advent of the internet marked another monumental transformation in our cognitive landscape. This vast network of interconnected computers has redefined how we communicate, share information, and learn. The internet broke down geographical barriers, enabling people to connect and collaborate regardless of their physical location. It fostered a culture of openness and exchange, where knowledge could flow freely among diverse communities. The internet has fundamentally altered our understanding of learning and interaction, empowering individuals to access a wealth of information and engage with others in ways that were previously unimaginable.

Algorithms can identify patterns, make predictions, and engage in basic problem-solving, providing powerful tools for decision-making. While these advancements showcase the potential of artificial intelligence, they also prompt critical questions about our reliance on machines for cognitive tasks. As we integrate cognitive technologies into our daily lives, it is essential to consider their implications for how we think, learn, and make decisions.

Throughout this evolution, the interplay between human and machine intelligence has remained a constant theme. Cognitive technologies have not replaced human thought but have instead complemented and enhanced it. The relationship between humans and their tools is reciprocal; as technology advances, so do our cognitive capabilities. By integrating cognitive technologies into our daily routines, we can focus on higher-order thinking, creativity, and problem-solving. By offloading routine tasks to machines, we free ourselves to explore innovative ideas and engage in critical thinking.

However, this evolution also brings to light important ethical and societal considerations. As cognitive technologies become increasingly embedded in our lives, we must contemplate how they influence our understanding of intelligence, creativity, and decision-making. The reliance on machines for cognitive processes raises questions about accountability, transparency, and potential biases. It is essential to ensure that cognitive technologies are developed and utilized in ways that prioritize ethical considerations and serve the common good.

Looking to the future, the potential for cognitive technologies to transform our lives is vast. Advancements in artificial intelligence and machine learning promise to revolutionize various fields, enhancing our understanding of complex challenges.

Ultimately, the growth of cognitive technologies is a testament to humanity's enduring pursuit of enhancement and understanding. From the earliest tools to the advanced systems we have today, this journey reflects our desire to push the boundaries of what is possible. As we continue to evolve alongside these technologies, we must remain vigilant in ensuring that they enrich our lives and elevate our collective intelligence. By embracing the potential of cognitive technologies while prioritizing ethical considerations, we can pave the way for a future where human and artificial intelligence coexist harmoniously, driving innovation and progress for generations to come.

Imagine a future where cognitive technologies are not just tools but co-creators in the intellectual journey. Could we witness a world where humans and machines together forge breakthroughs in fields like healthcare, climate science, or space exploration that would have been inconceivable on our own? The questions go beyond mere efficiency; they reach into the very core of how we define creativity, innovation, and human progress. As we expand our cognitive horizons with AI, will we still retain our individuality, or will we start to blur the lines between human and machine? The potential for these technologies to reshape our societies is vast. Yet, with these advancements comes a responsibility to consider their ethical implications. Are we prepared to ensure that this new partnership between human and machine remains aligned with our values, fostering trust and accountability? Can we create systems where cognitive technologies amplify human well-being, creativity, and societal good, or will the pursuit of progress sometimes lead us astray?

In conclusion, the narrative of cognitive technologies is one of discovery, collaboration, and transformation. As we reflect on this history, it is essential to recognize the profound impact these tools have had on shaping our societies and expanding our cognitive horizons. The journey continues, and as we stand at the crossroads of human and machine intelligence, we must embrace the possibilities ahead with curiosity, responsibility, and a commitment to creating a better future for all.

Real-Life Example: The Evolution of the Modern Calculator

The journey from pebbles to pocket-sized supercomputers is a testament to humanity's ingenuity. In ancient times, early humans used pebbles and abacuses to perform basic calculations—a humble beginning to what would become a revolution in computational tools. Fast-forward to 1967, when Texas Instruments unveiled the world's first handheld scientific calculator, forever changing the landscape of mathematics and science. For the first time, complex equations could be solved on the go, empowering scientists, students, and professionals alike. This groundbreaking device was more than a tool—it was a gateway to faster innovation, enabling humanity to tackle challenges with newfound precision and efficiency.

Why It Matters: Beyond convenience, the modern calculator symbolizes a larger trend: the continuous refinement of tools that amplify human potential. It's not just about crunching numbers faster—it's about opening doors to new realms of creativity, problem-solving, and exploration.

Analogy

Picture a world where traveling across a continent meant weeks on horseback. Then, imagine the awe when the first high-speed train sped onto the scene, shrinking the impossible into the achievable. The evolution of the calculator mirrors this leap. From the slow deliberation of manual counting to the lightning-fast computations of modern devices, the calculator has become an essential companion in our quest to solve the mysteries of the universe.

References:

- "The First Handheld Scientific Calculator" - TI Story: (https://education.ti.com/en/customer-support/about-timeline)

- Smithsonian: si.edu (https://www.si.edu)

Fun Fact:

The original pocket calculator, when it first came out, cost about $400 in today's money. Now, you can get the same functionality for free on any smartphone!

Humor:

Imagine trying to explain to someone in the 1800s that you use a "smartphone" to do your taxes—and also to throw birds at pigs during your breaks.

Future Vision:

Looking to the future, we might see cognitive technologies evolve from external tools into direct brain-computer interfaces. Imagine bypassing traditional input methods like keyboards or touchscreens and simply thinking your commands. You could complete tasks as soon as you think of them—no typing, no clicking—just pure cognitive interaction with machines.

1.3   The Role of Data and Algorithms in Enhancing Human Potential

In the dynamic landscape of modern life, the partnership between data and algorithms is transforming how we experience the world around us. This alliance is at the heart of artificial intelligence (AI) and is fundamentally reshaping our interactions, decisions, and overall human potential. As we delve into the intricacies of this relationship, we uncover how these elements not only fuel innovation but also enhance our capabilities, allowing us to navigate complexities with greater ease and insight.

The Ubiquity of Data

Every day, an immense amount of data is generated through various channels—social media interactions, online transactions, sensor readings, and countless other digital activities. This data forms the fabric of our contemporary existence, providing invaluable insights into human behavior, preferences, and trends. Yet, the sheer volume of data can often feel overwhelming. Understanding and harnessing this information requires more than just collecting it; it necessitates a thoughtful approach to its analysis and application.

Data in its raw form is like an unrefined resource. Just as crude oil must undergo refining to become usable fuel, data needs to be processed and analyzed to yield meaningful insights. This process begins with data collection, where various methods come into play to gather information effectively. Once collected, data must be cleaned, organized, and prepared for analysis. Here, algorithms enter the scene, acting as the vital tools that sift through the data, identifying patterns, anomalies, and correlations that might otherwise remain hidden.

The Power of Algorithms

Algorithms can be thought of as the recipes that guide the transformation of raw data into valuable insights. They provide a structured approach to processing information, allowing systems to learn and adapt over time. This adaptability is at the core of what makes AI so powerful. Algorithms can analyze complex datasets, uncovering trends and making predictions that are often beyond the capacity of human intuition alone.

Moreover, algorithms empower us to personalize our experiences. By analyzing our behaviors and preferences, they can curate content and recommendations that resonate with us individually. This personalization extends across various domains, from entertainment and shopping to healthcare and education. It fosters a more engaging experience, ensuring that the information and services we receive align closely with our unique needs.

Transforming Decision-Making

The intersection of data and algorithms is particularly evident in the realm of decision-making. In an age characterized by information overload, having access to precise insights can be a game-changer. Businesses, governments, and individuals increasingly rely on data-driven insights to inform their choices, leading to better outcomes and enhanced strategic planning.

For instance, organizations can analyze customer behavior and market trends to identify opportunities and threats. This data-driven approach allows them to pivot quickly, responding to shifts in consumer preferences and economic conditions. Such agility is essential in today's fast-paced environment, where the ability to adapt can determine the success or failure of an enterprise.

Fostering Creativity and Innovation

While data and algorithms enhance efficiency, they also spark creativity and innovation. By providing insights that were previously difficult to access, this powerful duo encourages individuals to think differently and explore new possibilities. The integration of data into the creative process allows for a richer exploration of ideas and concepts.

Partnership between human creativity and algorithmic analysis often leads to the emergence of innovative ideas and artistic expressions that challenge conventional norms.

Moreover, the iterative nature of working with data encourages experimentation. In entrepreneurship, the ability to quickly test concepts and refine them based on data-driven feedback is invaluable. This iterative process allows entrepreneurs to discover what resonates with their audience, ultimately leading to products and services that are more aligned with consumer needs.

Building Community and Connection

Beyond individual enhancement, the combination of data and algorithms has the power to build communities and foster connections. Social media platforms, powered by sophisticated algorithms, enable people to connect with others who share their interests, passions, and values. This interconnectedness creates a sense of belonging and community, allowing individuals to engage in meaningful discussions and collaborations.

Data-driven insights can also highlight social issues and disparities, prompting collective action and advocacy. Data-informed approach empowers individuals to make a difference, fostering a sense of agency and shared responsibility in tackling societal issues.

Navigating Ethical Considerations

As we harness the power of data and algorithms, it is crucial to remain vigilant about the ethical implications of these technologies. Data privacy, security, and algorithmic bias are pressing concerns that demand attention. As data collection becomes more ubiquitous, individuals must be aware of how their information is used and the potential consequences it may have on their lives.

Furthermore, algorithms are only as effective as the data they are trained on. Biases present in the data can lead to skewed algorithms, perpetuating inequalities and reinforcing stereotypes. It is vital for developers and organizations to prioritize fairness and transparency in their algorithms, ensuring that the benefits of AI are accessible to all, rather than a select few.

Maintaining a balance between human intuition and algorithmic analysis is essential. While algorithms can process vast amounts of information and identify patterns, they lack the emotional intelligence and ethical reasoning that humans possess. This balance ensures that technology enhances our capacity for empathy and moral judgment, rather than diminishing it.

Looking Toward the Future

As we gaze into the future, the relationship between data, algorithms, and human potential is poised for further evolution. The rapid pace of technological advancement suggests that we will continue to uncover new synergies between human and artificial intelligence. This future promises exciting possibilities, from enhanced problem-solving capabilities to deeper insights into the complexities of the human experience.

To fully embrace these opportunities, we must adopt a mindset of continuous learning and adaptation. As individuals and organizations, we must remain open to exploring new technologies and methodologies that can augment our capabilities. By leveraging data and algorithms as tools for empowerment, we unlock our full potential and contribute to a more innovative, equitable, and connected world.

In essence, the role of data and algorithms in enhancing human potential is multifaceted and profound. By transforming raw information into actionable insights, they empower individuals to make informed decisions, foster creativity, and build meaningful connections. As we navigate the complexities of the digital age, embracing the synergy between human intelligence and technology will be crucial in shaping a brighter future for all.

The journey of discovery, adaptation, and collaboration holds the promise of unlocking unprecedented levels of human potential, driving progress, and enriching our collective experience. Together, data and algorithms can illuminate the path ahead, guiding us toward new horizons where human ingenuity and technological advancement coexist harmoniously. In this evolving landscape, the partnership between data, algorithms, and human potential is not just a possibility; it is the foundation for a future brimming with potential, innovation, and connection.

Real-Life Example: Revolutionizing Agriculture with AI

Imagine a field where every drop of herbicide is purposefully applied—no waste, no guesswork. This is the reality created by AI-driven innovations like John Deere's "See & Spray" technology. Combining advanced data analytics and machine learning, this system can distinguish between crops and weeds in real time, delivering precision herbicide treatment only where it's needed. The result? A dramatic reduction in chemical use, significant cost savings for farmers, and a healthier environment for future generations. This isn't just farming; it's a technological revolution in sustainable agriculture.

Why It Matters: The implications of such innovations go far beyond the farm. By minimizing chemical runoff, this technology protects ecosystems and water supplies. It also empowers farmers to produce more with fewer resources, aligning agricultural practices with global sustainability goals. This is AI's promise in action—combining efficiency, innovation, and environmental stewardship to shape a better future.

Analogy

Think of this technology as a smart gardener. Instead of blindly watering an entire garden, it identifies and waters only the thirsty plants, leaving no drop wasted. Similarly, "See & Spray" ensures resources are used with pinpoint accuracy, transforming farming from a labor-intensive practice into a high-tech operation.

Reference:

- John Deere: John Deere Precision Ag Technology (https://www.deere.com/en/technology-products/precision-ag-technology)

- "John Deere See & Spray System" - Agronomist Journal (2021) (https://agronomyjournal.org)

Fun Fact:

John Deere's AI-powered tractors can spray herbicide with such precision that they reduce chemical usage by up to 90%. That's like giving a plant exactly the right amount of medicine with a dropper instead of flooding it with a bucket.

Humor:

Imagine a tractor so smart that it looks at your overgrown garden and says, "Don't worry, I've got this," while you sit back with a lemonade.

Future Vision:

As AI's ability to process data grows, we could see algorithms working alongside humans in more nuanced fields like mental health. AI could analyze massive datasets of human emotions, patterns of speech, or physiological markers to assist therapists in diagnosing and treating mental illnesses. In a world where algorithms understand human emotions as well as—or even better than—humans, we might even see AI working as a collaborative counselor, offering insights we couldn't perceive on our own.

1.4 How AI Shifts from Support to Collaboration in Intelligence

The landscape of artificial intelligence (AI) has changed dramatically over the years. Initially, AI was viewed primarily as a tool—something to automate repetitive tasks and assist with decision-making processes. However, as technology has evolved, so too has the role of AI in our lives. It has transitioned from being a mere support mechanism to becoming a collaborative partner, working alongside humans to enhance our cognitive abilities and reshape our understanding of intelligence. This transformation marks a significant shift in how we perceive the relationship between human and machine intelligence, and it carries profound implications for various fields, creativity, and the future of our collaboration with technology.

The Transition from Tool to Collaborator

In the beginning, AI was designed to handle simple, routine tasks. Think about the early days of computing, where the focus was on efficiency. Data entry, basic calculations, and other mundane tasks were the primary focus of AI applications. These early systems allowed humans to save time and effort, freeing them to engage in more complex responsibilities. But as technology progressed, it became evident that AI could do more than just follow instructions.

Now, we find ourselves in an era where AI systems are capable of working alongside humans in meaningful ways. In various sectors, from healthcare to finance, AI has evolved into a collaborative partner that enhances our capabilities rather than merely serving as a tool. This collaboration is transforming how we approach problems and innovate.

In the healthcare industry, AI has made remarkable strides. It no longer merely assists in data management; it plays an integral role in diagnosing illnesses and analyzing complex medical records. When medical professionals use AI to sift through vast amounts of data, they can gain insights that would be difficult to discern on their own. AI systems identify patterns and correlations in patient information that enhance the decision-making process. However, the human element remains crucial. Doctors bring their experience, intuition, and emotional intelligence into the equation, interpreting AI-generated insights to make informed decisions about patient care.

This collaboration enriches the medical field, enabling healthcare providers to deliver better outcomes for their patients. The fusion of AI's analytical prowess with human compassion creates a more effective and holistic approach to healthcare.

Legal Innovations through Collaboration

The legal sector is another area where AI's collaborative role is increasingly evident. Traditionally, lawyers relied on extensive research and documentation processes that consumed significant time and resources. Today, AI tools can streamline these tasks by quickly identifying relevant case precedents and analyzing legal documents. This allows lawyers to focus on the strategic aspects of their work, such as advocating for their clients and developing robust legal strategies.

In this context, AI acts as an assistant rather than a competitor. By handling the more labor-intensive aspects of legal research, AI empowers legal professionals to engage in higher-level thinking and problem-solving. This collaboration not only enhances productivity but also fosters innovation within the legal profession.

Creativity and AI: A New Frontier

The collaboration between AI and creative professionals is perhaps one of the most fascinating developments in recent years. Artists, musicians, and writers are beginning to view AI not just as a tool but as a creative partner. AI algorithms can analyze vast amounts of existing art, music, and literature, providing insights that inspire new works. This relationship has the potential to redefine creativity itself.

As creators experiment with AI-generated suggestions, they can push the boundaries of their own imagination. The synergy between human intuition and AI's computational capabilities opens up new avenues for artistic expression.

By collaborating with AI, artists can explore uncharted territories, resulting in innovative works that blend human emotion with machine intelligence.

Redefining Intelligence

The shift from AI as a support tool to a collaborative partner challenges our traditional understanding of intelligence. Historically, intelligence has been viewed as a distinctly human trait, characterized by reasoning, problem-solving, creativity, and emotional understanding. However, the emergence of AI as a collaborator blurs these boundaries, prompting us to rethink what intelligence means in a world where machines can enhance our cognitive abilities.

In this collaborative framework, intelligence becomes a shared resource. It is no longer solely about individual capabilities; it is an amalgamation of human creativity, emotional depth, and intuition, combined with AI's analytical skills and data processing abilities. This partnership enriches our decision-making processes, enabling us to tackle complex challenges with greater insight and effectiveness.

Driving Innovation through Collaboration

One of the most significant outcomes of this collaborative relationship is the acceleration of innovation. When humans and AI work together, they leverage their unique strengths to push the boundaries of what is possible. AI can quickly analyze vast datasets to identify emerging trends and opportunities, while humans can apply their insights and experiences to develop innovative solutions.

In research and development, this collaborative dynamic can lead to groundbreaking discoveries. Scientists can use AI to simulate experiments, analyze results, and even generate new hypotheses. By harnessing AI's computational power, researchers can explore uncharted territories and address complex questions that were previously beyond reach.

In business environments, collaboration between teams and AI tools fosters a culture of innovation. Employees are empowered to utilize AI for tasks such as market research and data analysis, allowing them to focus on strategic thinking and creative problem-solving. This shift encourages teams to explore new ideas, challenge conventional thinking, and develop solutions that address the evolving needs of their organizations and customers.

Ethical Considerations in Collaboration

As AI transitions from a supportive role to a collaborative partner, ethical considerations come to the forefront. The collaborative nature of AI raises important questions about accountability, bias, and the role of human oversight. While AI can enhance decision-making, it is essential to recognize that machines lack the moral and ethical frameworks that guide human behavior. Therefore, establishing guidelines to ensure AI operates transparently and fairly is crucial.

Bias in AI algorithms remains a pressing concern, as it can perpetuate inequalities and reinforce stereotypes. Collaborative frameworks must prioritize diversity and inclusion in the development of AI systems to mitigate these biases. By involving diverse stakeholders in the design and implementation of AI, we can create solutions that are more equitable and reflective of society as a whole.

Additionally, it lacks the emotional intelligence and ethical reasoning that humans possess. Striking a balance between AI's analytical capabilities and human judgment is essential to ensure that decisions made in collaboration are not only efficient but also ethically sound.

A Vision for the Future of Collaboration

As we look toward the future, the potential for collaboration between humans and AI is vast and largely untapped. As AI continues to evolve, we can expect to see even more sophisticated collaborations that transcend traditional boundaries. The next generation of AI systems may be designed to understand and respond to human emotions, enhancing their ability to collaborate in areas such as education, mental health, and customer service.

In education, AI-powered platforms could serve as personalized tutors, adapting to individual learning styles and needs. By collaborating with students, these AI systems can provide tailored feedback and support, fostering a deeper understanding of complex subjects. This partnership has the potential to revolutionize education, making learning more accessible and effective for all.

In the realm of mental health, AI could play a crucial role in providing support and resources. By analyzing patterns in individuals' behavior and emotional states, AI systems could offer insights and recommendations to mental health professionals, facilitating more effective treatment plans. This collaborative approach empowers individuals to take an active role in their mental health journey while providing professionals with valuable data to inform their practices.

A Shared Vision for Intelligence

The shift from AI as a mere support tool to a collaborative partner represents a profound transformation in our understanding of intelligence. As we embrace this evolution, it is crucial to foster a culture that values collaboration, ethical considerations, and inclusivity in AI development. By doing so, we can harness the full potential of this partnership to drive innovation, solve complex problems, and enhance human capabilities.

Ultimately, the journey toward a future where AI and humans collaborate seamlessly is a shared vision. It invites us to explore the limitless possibilities that arise when our unique strengths are combined. This partnership not only augments our intelligence but also enriches our experiences, enabling us to navigate the complexities of the world with greater insight, creativity, and purpose.

In this collaborative future, we have the opportunity to redefine what it means to be intelligent. It challenges us to expand our understanding of ourselves and our relationship with technology. By embracing AI as a collaborator rather than a competitor, we open the door to new horizons of possibility, innovation, and shared human experience. As we embark on this journey, we must remain committed to ethical practices, inclusivity, and the pursuit of knowledge that benefits all of humanity. Through collaboration, we can unlock the full potential of both human and artificial intelligence, creating a brighter and more equitable future for generations to come.

Real-Life Example: Redefining Legal Practice with AI

The legal profession, traditionally steeped in paperwork and meticulous research, is undergoing a quiet revolution, thanks to AI-driven tools like ROSS. Powered by IBM's Watson, ROSS is more than a digital librarian—it's a sophisticated legal assistant. It rapidly sifts through thousands of legal documents, interprets complex legal language, summarizes case law, and even predicts potential outcomes. By shouldering the heavy analytical workload, ROSS allows lawyers to shift their focus to what they do best: crafting strategies, negotiating outcomes, and delivering creative solutions for their clients.

Why It Matters: The impact of ROSS extends beyond efficiency. It democratizes access to legal resources by making complex research faster and more affordable. This technological shift empowers smaller law firms and solo practitioners to compete on a level playing field with larger firms, bridging the gap in access to justice. AI like ROSS doesn't replace lawyers—it enhances their capabilities, enabling them to focus on the human side of law.

Analogy

Imagine a seasoned detective paired with a high-tech AI assistant. While the detective focuses on connecting dots and solving the case, the AI tirelessly scans databases, uncovering leads and piecing together vital clues. This partnership amplifies efficiency and ensures no stone is left unturned, much like ROSS transforms the legal landscape by augmenting human expertise with AI precision.

Reference:

- ROSS Intelligence: (https://www.rossintelligence.com)
- IBM Watson in Law: (https://www.ibm.com/watson/legal)

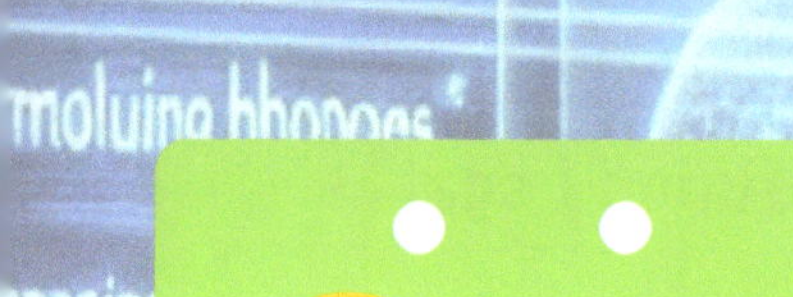

Fun Fact:

ROSS can analyze more than 1 billion text documents per second. That's faster than the time it takes most of us to even say the word "jurisprudence."

Humor:

Imagine telling a lawyer from the 1950s that in the future, their best assistant would be a machine with no law degree—but who still gives better legal advice than most interns.

Future Vision

The next step in AI collaboration might involve AI contributing to scientific research at the conceptual level. Picture AI systems formulating hypotheses and running virtual experiments, testing out thousands of variables at once. Rather than simply analyzing data, AI could co-lead breakthroughs in fields like physics or biology, helping to solve mysteries like dark matter or cracking the code of aging.

1.5   Milestones in the Co-Evolution of Humans and Machines

The intertwined narrative of human beings and machines unfolds like an epic saga, a journey defined by remarkable milestones that have fundamentally transformed the fabric of our existence. These milestones are not mere markers of technological progress; they are critical junctures that illustrate our evolving relationship with machines. As we reflect on this journey, we come to understand that each significant development has pushed the boundaries of human capabilities while simultaneously reshaping our society.

This relationship has roots that run deep, stretching back to the earliest days of human innovation. It is in this historical context that we can appreciate how far we have come, not just in terms of technology but also in how we define intelligence itself. The co-evolution of humans and machines is characterized by a series of transformative events that have enabled us to amplify our strengths and overcome our limitations.

The Birth of Computation

Our story begins with the birth of the first programmable computers, which set the stage for an entirely new realm of possibilities. These early machines, though rudimentary compared to today's technology, represented a monumental leap forward in our ability to solve complex problems. By allowing for the automation of calculations, these devices expanded our cognitive reach and enabled us to tackle challenges that had previously felt insurmountable. The invention of programming languages and algorithms laid the groundwork for a future where machines could perform tasks that once required human intellect and creativity.

The Emergence of Artificial Intelligence

As our understanding of computing deepened, the concept of artificial intelligence began to take shape. Researchers and pioneers began to explore the idea that machines could emulate human thought processes, leading to the birth of AI as a distinct field of study. This shift marked a critical milestone in our journey, revealing our desire to create systems that could learn, adapt, and improve over time.

The development of neural networks was a turning point in this narrative. Drawing inspiration from the human brain, these networks introduced a novel approach to information processing, enabling machines to recognize patterns and make decisions based on data. This leap in capability illuminated the potential for collaboration between human intuition and machine learning, fostering an environment ripe for innovation.

Machine Learning Revolution

With the maturation of machine learning, our relationship with machines evolved once more. This transformative technology allowed for the creation of systems capable of analyzing vast datasets and uncovering insights that would have taken humans an eternity to discover. The ability of these machines to learn from experience shifted the paradigm, allowing us to focus on higher-order thinking and creativity while leaving the heavy lifting of data analysis to intelligent systems.

As machine learning technologies advanced, the introduction of deep learning heralded another significant chapter in our story. With the capacity to handle complex tasks such as language processing and image recognition, deep learning systems began to reshape industries and redefine our interactions with technology. These advancements demonstrated the incredible potential of collaboration between human creativity and machine intelligence, paving the way for innovative applications that would change the landscape of everyday life.

The Integration of AI into Daily Life

The next milestone in this ongoing evolution was the seamless integration of AI technologies into our daily lives. From the rise of personal assistants to recommendation algorithms that tailor our experiences, AI began to permeate various aspects of our existence. This integration was not merely a technological shift; it represented a cultural transformation, altering how we interact with technology and with one another.

As AI systems became more sophisticated, they began to play an integral role in decision-making processes across various sectors. The ability to analyze real-time data and provide insights revolutionized everything from healthcare to finance, leading to smarter, more efficient operations. This dynamic shift illustrated the profound impact of human-machine collaboration, showcasing the potential for technology to enhance our lives rather than simply serve as a tool.

The Creative Fusion of Human and Machine

One of the most captivating developments in our co-evolution has been the fusion of human creativity with machine intelligence. As AI systems began to generate original content, artists, musicians, and writers started to see machines not as competitors but as collaborators. This collaborative spirit opened new avenues for artistic expression, challenging traditional notions of creativity and authorship.

In this context, the blending of human emotion and machine-generated ideas has led to rich and diverse outcomes. The interplay between human creativity and machine learning encourages a deeper exploration of what it means to create, innovate, and express oneself. As we navigate this fascinating landscape, it becomes evident that the partnership between humans and machines can yield extraordinary results that neither could achieve independently.

Ethical Considerations in Co-Evolution

However, as we celebrate these milestones, it is crucial to acknowledge the ethical considerations that accompany our increasingly intertwined relationship with machines. The rapid advancement of AI has raised important questions regarding accountability, bias, and the potential for misuse. As machines take on more significant roles in our lives, it is imperative that we establish ethical frameworks that prioritize fairness, transparency, and responsibility.

Addressing these ethical challenges is not just a responsibility but a vital aspect of our journey together. As we continue to develop and integrate AI technologies, we must remain vigilant in mitigating potential biases and ensuring equitable access to the benefits of AI. The responsibility lies with us to shape a future where human dignity and machine intelligence coexist harmoniously, fostering an environment that enhances our collective potential.

Envisioning the Future of Co-Evolution

As we reflect on the milestones we have achieved in the co-evolution of humans and machines, we find ourselves standing on the threshold of an exciting future. The possibilities that lie ahead are vast, and as we continue to explore the potential of AI, we must remain committed to nurturing this partnership.

The future promises even more sophisticated forms of collaboration, as AI systems become increasingly adept at understanding human emotions and intentions. This shift holds the potential to create a more intuitive and empathetic partnership, allowing for deeper connections between humans and machines. As we embrace this evolution, we must also consider the societal implications of our choices, ensuring that our advancements align with our shared values and aspirations.

Moreover, as we harness the power of AI to address complex global challenges, the significance of co-evolution will be more critical than ever. By combining human creativity and problem-solving skills with the analytical capabilities of AI, we can forge solutions that have a meaningful impact on society. The partnership between humans and machines can serve as a catalyst for innovation, driving progress in areas that require urgent attention and collaboration.

The Importance of the Human Experience

At the core of this co-evolution is our shared human experience. As technology continues to advance, it is essential to remain grounded in the values that define us as a species. The milestones we achieve must reflect our commitment to improving the human condition and fostering a world where technology enhances human potential rather than replaces it.

Navigating this dynamic landscape requires a balance between embracing change and upholding ethical principles. The co-evolution of humans and machines is not merely a technological journey; it is a profound cultural and societal transformation that will shape the trajectory of our future. As we explore this new terrain, we must strive to cultivate a relationship with technology that reflects our highest aspirations.

Conclusion: A Shared Journey Forward

In conclusion, the milestones in the co-evolution of humans and machines tell a story of remarkable progress and endless possibilities. Each significant development serves as a reminder of our incredible journey—one characterized by collaboration, innovation, and the pursuit of a shared vision for a better world. As we continue to write this narrative, let us remain dedicated to nurturing the partnership between human and machine intelligence, striving for a future that reflects our collective potential and shared values.

This journey is far from over; it is a continuous evolution where each milestone brings us closer to a world where intelligence—both human and artificial—can thrive together. Embracing this co-evolution will not only enrich our lives but also illuminate the path toward a brighter future, one where the synergy between humans and machines empowers us to reach new heights of creativity, understanding, and achievement.

Real-Life Example: GPT-3 and the Evolution of Linguistic Intelligence

The arrival of OpenAI's GPT-3 marked a new era in artificial intelligence, one where machines could seemingly hold a conversation, craft poetry, and compose essays that rival human writing. With its ability to engage in philosophical debates and generate text that feels almost human, GPT-3 has pushed the boundaries of what language models can achieve. However, despite its impressive linguistic prowess, GPT-3 is not a sentient writer—it relies on vast amounts of data and human oversight to ensure its outputs are coherent, meaningful, and contextually relevant.

Why It Matters: GPT-3's capabilities have sparked debates about the nature of creativity itself. Can a machine that mimics human language and ideas be truly creative? While it may not replace human ingenuity, GPT-3 exemplifies how AI can amplify human creativity by handling the heavy lifting of routine tasks, leaving humans free to focus on innovation and strategic thinking. This collaboration between human insight and machine efficiency is the essence of AI's transformative potential.

Analogy

Picture GPT-3 as a virtuoso pianist who has mastered every note and technique but depends on a conductor to guide the performance. While the pianist dazzles with technical skill, the conductor ensures the music resonates with emotion and intent. Similarly, GPT-3 can create text with remarkable fluency, but human input ensures it aligns with the desired message and purpose.

Reference:

- OpenAI GPT-3 Overview: (https://openai.com/research/gpt-3)
- "Language Models are Few-Shot Learners" - *OpenAI Blog* (2020) (https://arxiv.org/abs/2005.14165)

Fun Fact:

GPT-3 has been used to write short stories, blogs, and even compose music. It's the first AI to successfully ghostwrite an entire book! So, if you've got writer's block, GPT-3 could step in and help.

Humor:

Can you imagine Shakespeare having GPT-3 as a writing partner? "To be, or not to be... uh, GPT-3, can you finish that line?"

Future Vision:

The co-evolution of humans and machines is heading toward even deeper integration. Imagine a future where AI co-inventors are listed on patents, or where humans and machines collaborate to create entirely new fields of art, science, and literature. In the medical field, machines could collaborate with humans to design new drugs or personalized medical treatments based on real-time genetic analysis. The milestones of the future will involve AI not just working for humans, but co-evolving with us to push the boundaries of what's possible for both biological and machine intelligence.

Chapter 2

Creative Fusion

In recent years, artificial intelligence (AI) has evolved far beyond its initial perception as merely a tool for enhancing productivity. Instead, it has emerged as a dynamic catalyst for human creativity. This transformation is profound, as it redefines not just how we create but also how we understand the very essence of creativity itself. The intersection of human imagination and machine capability is reshaping the landscape of artistic and innovative expression, inviting us to explore the boundless potential of this collaboration.

Creativity is often regarded as an inherently human trait, closely tied to our emotions, experiences, and the ability to dream. It encompasses a vast array of activities, from composing music to designing products, and it flourishes in an environment that encourages exploration and risk-taking. However, traditional notions of creativity often overlook the potential for enhancement through external influences. This is where AI steps in, offering a fresh perspective that encourages us to rethink our approach to creative endeavors.

At its core, AI possesses remarkable abilities that can significantly amplify human creativity. It can process enormous volumes of data, recognize patterns, and generate original ideas at a speed and scale that far surpasses human capability. This analytical prowess opens up new avenues for exploration, allowing artists, writers, musicians, and innovators to tap into a reservoir of insights that were previously hidden from view. When we harness these capabilities, we find ourselves standing at the threshold of a new creative era, where possibilities abound.

One of the most remarkable aspects of AI's contribution to creativity is its capacity to generate original content. While some may view this as a threat to traditional forms of artistic expression, it is essential to recognize that AI-generated outputs are not replacements for human creativity; they are enhancements. Imagine an artist who collaborates with an AI program that can generate novel visual concepts. The AI might propose unexpected color palettes or forms that the artist might never have considered. This collaboration enriches the creative process, prompting the artist to explore uncharted territories in their work.

Moreover, AI can alleviate the burden of technical and repetitive tasks that often bog down the creative process. Many creators find themselves caught in the minutiae of their craft—whether it's editing, formatting, or managing details that detract from their ability to focus on the essence of their work. AI can take on these roles, allowing creators to devote their time and energy to what truly matters: innovation and expression. By automating the more tedious aspects of creative work, AI enables individuals to dive deeper into their creative processes and pursue ideas that resonate with their true vision.

This partnership between humans and AI also fosters an environment ripe for collaboration. The act of creation has always thrived on the exchange of ideas, whether between individuals or across disciplines. With AI as a collaborator, human creators can engage in a dynamic interplay of inspiration and feedback. The AI system might suggest concepts, analyze past works, or simulate various outcomes, prompting the human creator to refine their vision and expand their horizons. This synergy between human intuition and machine intelligence creates fertile ground for innovation, where new ideas can blossom and flourish.

Furthermore, the democratization of creativity brought about by AI is noteworthy. Historically, access to creative tools and resources has often been restricted by factors such as cost, expertise, and availability. However, as AI technologies become increasingly user-friendly and accessible, more individuals are empowered to engage in creative pursuits. A person without formal training in music composition can use AI-powered tools to experiment with melodies, while aspiring writers can harness algorithms to generate story ideas. This democratization opens doors for diverse voices and perspectives, enriching the cultural tapestry and fostering a more inclusive creative community.

As we continue to explore the transformative role of AI in creativity, it is crucial to approach this partnership with mindfulness and responsibility. The ethical implications surrounding AI's use must be carefully considered. Concerns such as algorithmic bias, the authenticity of AI-generated content, and the potential impact on traditional artistic forms warrant thoughtful examination. It is vital to ensure that the creative process remains respectful of individual expression and does not inadvertently perpetuate harmful stereotypes or exclusionary practices.

Despite AI's impressive capabilities, **it is important to recognize that human creativity is irreplaceable.** While AI can generate ideas and facilitate collaboration, it lacks the emotional depth, empathy, and lived experiences that define the human experience. The most compelling creative works resonate with audiences on a profound level, evoking emotions and fostering connection. As we embrace AI's potential, we must remain vigilant in preserving the unique qualities that make human creativity so special.

The synergy between human and machine creativity ultimately challenges us to reconsider our definitions of art and innovation. In a world where AI can contribute to creative processes, we find ourselves in an era of hybrid creativity—one that marries human intuition with machine intelligence. This new paradigm not only expands the boundaries of what is possible but also invites us to explore deeper questions about the nature of creativity itself. What does it mean to create? How do we define authorship in a collaborative landscape? These inquiries prompt us to reflect on the essence of artistic expression and the roles we play within it.

In conclusion, AI's role as a catalyst for human creativity is a powerful force in our evolving cultural narrative. By processing vast amounts of data, generating original content, and automating repetitive tasks, AI empowers human creators to unlock new realms of artistic expression. This partnership between human and machine fosters innovation, collaboration, and inclusivity, pushing the boundaries of what we can achieve together. As we navigate this exciting landscape, we must embrace the potential of AI while remaining grounded in the values that define human creativity. The future of creativity lies in our ability to forge meaningful connections between human intuition and machine intelligence, ultimately enriching our artistic endeavors and expanding the horizons of human expression.

As we move forward into this new creative era, we are not simply passive observers; we are active participants in shaping a world where creativity knows no bounds. AI invites us to dream bigger, think differently, and explore the uncharted territories of our imagination. Together, we are embarking on a journey that transcends traditional boundaries and redefines what it means to be creative in a world where human ingenuity and artificial intelligence coexist in harmony.

Real-Life Example: Reimagining Genius with "The Next Rembrandt"

What if an artist who lived 350 years ago could create something new today? That's exactly what "The Next Rembrandt" project sought to achieve using AI. By meticulously analyzing 346 of Rembrandt van Rijn's masterpieces, the AI learned his signature brushstrokes, color palette, and intricate techniques for rendering facial expressions. The result? A painting so true to Rembrandt's style that it could have emerged from his own hand. While the Dutch master remains irreplaceable, this groundbreaking project demonstrates how AI can bring the past to life, reimagining creativity in ways once thought impossible.

Why It Matters: "The Next Rembrandt" is more than a technical feat—it's a philosophical exploration of creativity. It challenges us to consider how technology can complement human artistry rather than compete with it. By enabling modern creators to interact with the styles and techniques of history's greats, AI transforms itself into a tool of inspiration and collaboration, enriching the creative process in unprecedented ways.

Analogy

Imagine a symphony where AI serves as the orchestra, playing with technical precision, while the conductor embodies the soul of Rembrandt, guiding every note to evoke his timeless genius. This collaboration doesn't replace the artist but amplifies and honors his work, creating a harmony that bridges history and innovation.

Reference:

- The Next Rembrandt" AI Painting: (https://www.nextrembrandt.com)
- "How a Team Used AI to Create a New Rembrandt"
  - *The Verge* (2016) (https://www.theverge.com)

Fun Fact:

The AI behind "The Next Rembrandt" analyzed over 168,000 fragments of Rembrandt's work. That's like analyzing every brushstroke of every painting in the Louvre—in just a few seconds.

Humor:

Imagine AI telling Rembrandt, "I think I've nailed your style, but next time, maybe throw in some neon colors and a cat meme for the modern crowd."

Future Vision:

In the future, we may see AI working alongside human artists to create collaborative masterpieces. Imagine walking into a gallery and seeing a painting that was co-created by a human artist and an AI. The AI might generate the foundational structure, and the human artist could add the final, creative touches. Together, they'd form a dynamic duo that pushes the boundaries of both human and machine creativity.

2.2   Merging Human Intuition with AI's Pattern Recognition

Human intuition is a captivating element of our cognitive landscape. It's that inexplicable feeling, that instinctive understanding, which often guides us through complex decisions. Think of those moments when you sense a colleague is struggling despite their outward calm or when you instinctively know which project to pursue next. This innate ability allows us to navigate life's uncertainties, relying on a blend of experiences, emotions, and subconscious cues that inform our choices. While many have come to view intuition as a uniquely human trait, its power becomes even more profound when combined with the analytical strengths of artificial intelligence.

The interplay between human intuition and AI's pattern recognition creates a dynamic partnership with the potential to transform problem-solving across various domains. When these two forces unite, the results can be extraordinary, enhancing our ability to make informed decisions and uncover innovative solutions to complex challenges. Intuition can steer AI in the right direction, guiding it toward areas of interest and significance. In turn, AI can offer insights and analyses that empower human intuition, leading to more nuanced and informed choices.

Consider how this collaboration can manifest in healthcare. Doctors often rely on their gut feelings when diagnosing patients, drawing from their experiences and instincts to guide their assessments. However, the complexity of medical data can be overwhelming. By integrating AI's capabilities to analyze patient histories, clinical data, and treatment outcomes, healthcare providers can gain deeper insights that bolster their intuitive judgments. This synergy not only enhances diagnostic accuracy but also improves patient care.

In the business world, the fusion of human intuition and AI analytics can revolutionize decision-making. Business leaders often sense shifts in market trends or consumer behavior based on their instincts and experiences. When these insights are coupled with AI's ability to process customer data and identify emerging patterns, companies can create strategies that resonate with their audiences more effectively. This collaboration allows businesses to remain agile and responsive in a competitive landscape, driving innovation and success.

The creative industries also stand to benefit from this merging of capabilities. Artists, writers, and musicians often rely on intuition to fuel their creativity, tapping into emotions and experiences that shape their work. AI, with its analytical strengths, can support this creative process by providing insights into trends and styles. Imagine an artist creating a piece driven by emotion, while AI analyzes visual trends to suggest complementary color schemes or techniques. This blending of human insight and machine learning can lead to groundbreaking artistic expressions that challenge conventional boundaries.

Furthermore, the combination of human intuition and AI's analytical capabilities can enhance ethical decision-making. In scenarios that involve complex moral dilemmas, AI can present data-driven insights that outline the consequences of various actions. At the same time, human intuition can weigh the ethical implications of those outcomes, ensuring that decisions reflect core values and social responsibility. This integrated approach fosters a decision-making framework that is not only effective but also principled.

As we look toward the future, the merging of human intuition with AI's pattern recognition capabilities is poised to grow even more significant. The relentless advancement of AI technologies, paired with our deepening understanding of human cognition, suggests a future where the synergy between these two forces is even more pronounced. Individuals and organizations that embrace this collaboration will be better equipped to navigate the complexities of modern life, addressing challenges that demand both analytical precision and human insight.

In this evolving landscape, the potential for growth and exploration is immense. By harnessing the strengths of both human intuition and AI, we can unlock new possibilities for innovation and problem-solving. This partnership enriches our understanding of the world around us, allowing us to tackle complex issues with greater confidence and creativity.

Ultimately, the merger of human intuition and AI's pattern recognition stands as a testament to what can be achieved when we recognize and leverage the strengths of both. This collaboration opens doors to innovative solutions that neither could achieve alone, creating a richer tapestry of insights and possibilities.

Real-Life Example: Personalizing Fashion with AI

In the world of fashion, personalization is key—and companies like Stitch Fix are leveraging AI to take this to the next level. By analyzing customer preferences, body types, and the latest trends, AI generates tailored clothing recommendations that resonate with individual tastes. But the magic doesn't stop there. Human stylists play a crucial role in reviewing these suggestions, using their intuition and creativity to ensure the final choices feel just right. This seamless blending of human insight with AI's analytical power results in a shopping experience that's not only efficient but deeply personal.

Why It Matters: This collaboration showcases the future of consumer experiences—one where technology doesn't replace human touch but enhances it. By automating the heavy lifting of data analysis, AI allows stylists to focus on building a deeper connection with customers. The result is a win-win: customers enjoy a more personalized wardrobe, while stylists get to spend more time on the art of styling, rather than sifting through data.

Analogy

Think of this process as a duet between a skilled pianist and an advanced player piano. The piano handles the technical, precise execution of the music, but the pianist adds emotion, subtlety, and personal flair. Similarly, Stitch Fix's AI handles the data-heavy analysis, while human stylists infuse the recommendations with empathy and style.

Reference –

- Stitch Fix's AI:(https://www.stitchfix.com)
- "How Stitch Fix Uses AI to Help Personalize Your Wardrobe" - *Wired* (2019) (https://www.wired.com/story/how-stitch-fix-uses-ai-help-personalize-your-wardrobe/)

Fun Fact:

AI can scan fashion trends from thousands of websites in a fraction of a second. Yet, it still needs a human touch to figure out why wearing socks with sandals never caught on.

Humor:

Imagine an AI fashion stylist suggesting, "How about a neon green jumpsuit with a velvet cape?" And the human stylist replies, "We're aiming for chic, not superhero!"

Future Vision:

Looking ahead, the fusion of human intuition and AI's pattern recognition could lead to more advanced, personalized experiences in other fields as well. Imagine an AI psychologist that analyzes a patient's speech patterns and body language while a human therapist uses intuition and empathy to guide the conversation. This could lead to more precise and effective mental health treatments, blending the analytical power of AI with the emotional intelligence of humans.

2.3   The Future of Creative Problem-Solving through HumIntel

HumIntel—the merging of human and artificial intelligence—marks the dawn of a new era in how we approach problem-solving. While AI excels at processing large amounts of data, identifying patterns, and executing tasks with speed and precision, humans bring irreplaceable qualities to the table: imagination, emotional understanding, and the ability to think abstractly. When these strengths are brought together, the potential for solving complex and creative challenges grows beyond what either could accomplish alone.

In this evolving landscape, HumIntel has the power to transform how we tackle difficult problems. By combining the analytical capacity of AI with the ingenuity of human thought, new possibilities emerge. It is not just about automating processes or analyzing data faster; it's about enhancing our ability to think outside the box, to find solutions that blend logic with creativity, precision with empathy. This hybrid approach unlocks doors to innovations that were previously out of reach.

The secret to shaping this future lies in **true collaboration**—where AI handles the heavy lifting in areas it excels, and humans inject the process with intuition, creativity, and emotional wisdom. By blending these strengths, we move past the limits of what either can achieve alone, creating a powerful synergy that transforms how we think, solve problems, and dream up new possibilities. It's not just about working together; it's about unlocking a whole new level of innovation, where human insight and machine precision merge to shape a future, we've only begun to imagine.

HumIntel doesn't just improve problem-solving—it revolutionizes it. By fusing the unique strengths of human intuition with the speed and precision of artificial intelligence, we're not simply enhancing our capabilities; we're rewriting the rules of innovation itself. This seamless partnership between human creativity and machine intelligence unleashes a dynamic force that allows us to tackle challenges in ways never thought possible. We're on the brink of breakthroughs that will transform industries, reshape societies, and redefine what's achievable. With HumIntel, the future isn't just imagined—it's created, one groundbreaking solution at a time.

Real-Life Example: Revolutionizing Cancer Treatment with AI

A groundbreaking example of AI's transformative potential can be seen in the work of companies like Atomwise, which is using artificial intelligence to revolutionize the search for cancer treatments. Atomwise's AI technology analyzes millions of chemical compounds, predicting their effectiveness in targeting cancer cells. This powerful system identifies promising drug candidates in a fraction of the time it would take traditional methods. After AI narrows down the possibilities, human researchers step in to conduct preclinical and clinical trials. This fusion of AI's speed and human expertise is accelerating the discovery of life-saving cancer therapies, with the potential to treat cancers that were previously deemed untreatable.

Why It Matters: AI's ability to rapidly sift through vast chemical landscapes is dramatically reducing the time required for drug discovery. In cancer research, where every second counts, this speed and precision could make the difference between life and death for patients. The power of AI to uncover hidden opportunities is setting the stage for faster, more effective treatments for a disease that has long been a major challenge in medicine.

Analogy

Think of AI as a high-powered microscope that sifts through countless molecules to find the one that can best target a cancerous cell. Once the right molecule is identified, human researchers take the role of a skilled surgeon, carefully applying their knowledge and experience to bring the solution to life. Together, AI and humans are dissecting the problem and piecing together the cure.

Reference:

- Atomwise: atomwise.com
- "How AI is Transforming the Search for Cancer Drugs" – *Nature Medicine* (2021)

Fun Fact:

AI can generate a new drug candidate in less than a day, whereas traditional drug discovery methods can take years.

Humor:

Imagine AI coming up with a miracle drug and a human scientist saying, "Great job! But next time, let's avoid creating something that turns people into zombies."

Future Vision:

The future of creative problem-solving through HumIntel could lead to a world where humans and AI collaborate in every aspect of life. Picture a world where AI helps architects design sustainable cities, and human intuition refines the designs to create spaces that are not only efficient but also beautiful. We could see HumIntel being applied to global challenges like climate change, where AI predicts environmental trends, and humans craft creative policies to address them. This partnership could make problem-solving faster, more efficient, and far more imaginative.

2.4   How Machine Learning Enhances Artistic and Scientific Pursuits

Machine learning is reshaping the landscape of creativity and scientific discovery in ways we are only beginning to grasp. As a powerful subset of artificial intelligence, machine learning acts as a dynamic partner in both the artistic and scientific communities, enhancing the capabilities of individuals and pushing the boundaries of what can be achieved.

In the realm of art, the marriage of machine learning and creativity is sparking a revolution. Artists today are no longer confined to traditional methods; they can now engage with algorithms that have been trained on a rich tapestry of styles, techniques, and historical contexts. This fusion creates a unique opportunity for artists to collaborate with technology, generating works that reflect a stunning blend of human emotion and machine precision. Artists can feed their visions into algorithms, which analyze existing pieces and synthesize new ideas that resonate with their creative intent.

This collaboration does not seek to replace the artist but instead amplifies their creative voice. Imagine an artist exploring uncharted territories, where the possibilities are as vast as their imagination. Machine learning tools empower artists to experiment, enabling them to discover new color palettes, brush strokes, and compositions that might not have emerged through conventional methods. By analyzing patterns in existing artworks, algorithms can suggest novel approaches, igniting inspiration and opening doors to innovative techniques.

The process becomes a dialogue, where the artist's intuition and emotional depth converge with the analytical prowess of machine learning. This interaction fosters an environment rich in experimentation, encouraging artists to take risks and explore unorthodox ideas. As they navigate this new landscape, artists find themselves not just as creators but as co-creators, engaging with a digital collaborator that enhances their unique vision.

On the scientific front, machine learning is ushering in a new era of discovery. Scientists are confronted with an overwhelming amount of data, often too vast for traditional analysis methods. Here, machine learning shines, demonstrating its ability to sift through mountains of information, identify hidden patterns, and generate insights that would take human researchers years to uncover. This capacity for rapid data analysis accelerates the research process, enabling scientists to generate hypotheses and draw conclusions more efficiently.

By harnessing machine learning, researchers can focus their energies on the creative aspects of science: developing new theories, designing experiments, and interpreting results. The technology handles the heavy lifting of data processing, allowing scientists to delve deeper into the nuances of their fields. As a result, the boundaries of scientific inquiry expand, making it possible to explore phenomena that were once thought to be beyond reach.

The interplay between human creativity and machine learning nurtures a profound appreciation for the processes inherent in both art and science. Artists engaging with algorithms discover patterns that illuminate their craft, while scientists recognize the artistry involved in forming hypotheses and conducting research. This recognition fosters a culture where creativity and analysis are not seen as opposing forces but as complementary elements driving innovation.

As we move forward into a future where machine learning continues to evolve, its role as a catalyst in both artistic and scientific pursuits becomes increasingly significant. This partnership embodies the idea that technology can be a tool for enhancement rather than replacement. It encourages a collaborative spirit, one where human intuition and machine precision work in harmony, unlocking new realms of exploration and expression.

Moreover, the relationship between machine learning and these fields cultivates a community of thinkers who are unafraid to challenge conventions. Artists are inspired to push boundaries, while scientists are emboldened to tackle complex questions. The synergy created by machine learning enriches both communities, leading to innovative practices that redefine what it means to create and discover.

Real-Life Example: AI-Driven Art and Scientific Breakthroughs

AI is making waves is in the realm of science, particularly with DeepMind's AlphaFold. This AI system has cracked one of the biggest mysteries in molecular biology: predicting the 3D structure of proteins. Understanding how proteins fold is crucial to unlocking solutions for diseases like Alzheimer's and cancer. Thanks to AlphaFold, this breakthrough has opened up new possibilities for drug development and disease treatment, dramatically accelerating progress in the field of biology.

Why It Matters: The ability to predict protein structures is a game-changer in biotechnology, offering hope for faster and more effective treatments for a range of diseases. This AI breakthrough not only marks a leap forward in scientific discovery but also demonstrates how machine learning can solve some of the world's most complex problems.

Analogy

Think of AlphaFold as a puzzle solver, capable of assembling intricate molecular pieces into a complete picture. By putting these pieces together, it helps scientists unlock the hidden secrets of biology, providing them with a map to guide future research and treatment.

References:

- DeepMind: (https://www.deepmind.com)
- "How AlphaFold Is Revolutionizing Biology" – Nature (2021) (https://www.nature.com)

Fun Fact:

DeepMind's AlphaFold can predict the structure of proteins with 90% accuracy, a task that used to take scientists years, if not decades, to accomplish manually.

Humor:

Imagine an AI trying to paint a portrait and getting stuck on abstract shapes, while the human artist says, "Uh, thanks, but I was going for a landscape."

Future Vision:

In the future, machine learning could enhance both artistic and scientific pursuits in even more profound ways. Imagine AI helping musicians compose symphonies by analyzing thousands of classical pieces and suggesting novel chord progressions. In science, machine learning could assist researchers by running millions of virtual experiments overnight, providing scientists with a shortlist of promising ideas by the time they have their morning coffee. The intersection of AI and human creativity will likely lead to a golden age of discovery and innovation.

2.5   Case Studies: AI and Human Partnerships in Creative Fields

The fusion of artificial intelligence (AI) with human creativity is dramatically reshaping the arts, opening up new horizons for expression and innovation. Whether in film, fashion, visual arts, or other creative industries, AI is becoming an essential collaborator, not a replacement, empowering human creators to explore new dimensions of their craft. Through real-life examples, we see how this synergy is changing the landscape, sparking innovation, and challenging traditional boundaries.

1. The Transformation of Filmmaking: Redefining Storytelling

In filmmaking, AI is not just a tool; it's a collaborator that helps filmmakers tell more engaging, tailored stories. One prime example is the film Morgan (2016), where IBM's Watson was employed to analyze thousands of horror movie trailers to create its own trailer for the film. This was a groundbreaking move, showing AI's capacity to analyze emotion, pacing, and tone to generate creative outputs.

Beyond this, AI is now routinely used to analyze vast amounts of data, such as past film performances, audience preferences, and script elements, helping studios make informed decisions. Directors like Jordan Peele have spoken about using AI-driven data to understand audience reactions better. This blend of machine learning and human intuition has revolutionized how scripts are refined, casting decisions are made, and narratives are shaped.

Case Study: 20th Century Fox worked with AI to predict audience engagement for their 2019 film Ad Astra. By analyzing trailers and audience data, they optimized their marketing strategy to target demographics with the highest engagement potential, boosting box office success.

2. Fashion: Revolutionizing Design and Consumer Experience

Fashion has embraced AI to both inform and inspire design. AI tools are now capable of analyzing social media trends, past sales, and fashion show data to predict what will be "in" next season. Companies like Stitch Fix use

AI to recommend personalized clothing choices to customers, blending style preferences with advanced algorithms to create tailored fashion selections.

On the design front, AI helps creatives like Tommy Hilfiger, who partnered with IBM and the Fashion Institute of Technology to build a system that analyzed fashion trends and customer preferences. Designers used these insights to develop collections that combined current trends with futuristic flair, turning data into inspiration.

Additionally, AI is enhancing consumer engagement through innovations like virtual fitting rooms and AR shopping experiences. Zara has introduced AI-powered mirrors that recommend outfits based on the customer's current selections, reshaping the in-store experience. This technology blends human creativity with AI's ability to analyze patterns, personalizing the fashion experience.

3. Music: AI as a Creative Partner

In the music industry, AI is being used to compose music, assist in production, and provide real-time creative inputs. Artists like Taryn Southern have composed entire albums with AI. Her album I AM AI (2017) was one of the first to use AI as a core collaborator, blending human emotion with machine-driven composition.

AI systems like OpenAI's Jukedeck and Aiva use neural networks to compose original tracks, while musicians retain creative control, deciding how the AI's suggestions are incorporated into their work. For instance, AI can analyze song structures to recommend harmonic changes or create completely new sounds, pushing musical creativity into uncharted territories.

Case Study: Composer David Cope developed a system called Experiments in Musical Intelligence, which has been used to create music in the style of classical composers like Bach and Beethoven, blurring the lines between human creativity and machine-generated music.

4. Visual Arts: Expanding Creative Boundaries

In the visual arts, AI is changing how artists create, curate, and conserve their work. Generative art, which uses algorithms to produce pieces based on specific parameters, is giving rise to a new art movement. Artists like Refik Anadol have used AI to create large-scale installations that visualize data in visually stunning, abstract forms.

AI-generated art is not just a technical feat—it's a fresh way of exploring visual aesthetics. Anadol's piece Machine Hallucination explores how AI interprets thousands of images to create a new, machine-driven form of artistic expression. His use of AI challenges our understanding of creativity, questioning the relationship between artist and tool.

Moreover, AI plays a vital role in art restoration and preservation. Tools like Art Recognition use AI to authenticate artworks by analyzing brushstrokes and detecting forgeries, preserving cultural heritage. These tools are invaluable for both galleries and collectors, blending AI's precision with human expertise to safeguard artistic integrity.

Case Study: Sotheby's made headlines in 2018 when it auctioned the AI-generated artwork Portrait of Edmond de Belamy, created by the collective Obvious. The piece sold for $432,500, challenging the notion of what constitutes art and who (or what) is the creator.

5. Architecture and Design: From Concept to Creation

Architecture and design are fields where AI is rapidly becoming a co-creator. AI-driven tools like Spacemaker AI assist architects in optimizing design plans by considering environmental factors, space use, and energy efficiency. This collaboration not only speeds up the design process but also leads to more sustainable, functional structures.

Renowned architect Zaha Hadid incorporated AI and algorithmic design processes in her projects, pushing architectural boundaries. By using AI to explore complex forms and dynamic structures, Hadid's work showcased a futuristic vision, blending human creativity with machine precision.

AI also plays a critical role in generating complex, parametric designs that would be nearly impossible to conceptualize manually. These tools provide real-time feedback, enabling architects to iterate designs swiftly, making the creative process more efficient and innovative.

Real-Life Example: AI and Human Creativity in Architecture

A striking example of AI's transformative impact can be seen in the design of the Dubai Opera House. In this groundbreaking project, architects employed AI-driven modeling to predict crowd flow, optimize the building's acoustics, and fine-tune its aesthetic design. The goal was to create not only a visually stunning landmark but also a functional space that would deliver an unparalleled auditory experience. AI helped balance the complex requirements of crowd movement and sound quality, making sure that the grand design was not just an architectural marvel but also a space where every note could be heard with precision.

Why It Matters: This case highlights how AI is helping architects achieve an equilibrium between artistic vision and technical performance. By simulating real-world conditions and providing data-driven insights, AI is no longer just a tool; it's a collaborator in the creative process, enabling us to push the boundaries of what's possible in design.

References: AI tools have been used in architectural projects for optimization (crowd flow, acoustics, and aesthetics).

Analogy

Imagine the Dubai Opera House as a symphony—each element, from crowd flow to acoustics, is a different instrument. While human architects compose the score, AI acts as the conductor, ensuring that every section plays in harmony to create a flawless performance. The result is a building that's not just a work of art, but a perfectly orchestrated experience.

Fun Fact:

The AI used by Zaha Hadid Architects can analyze thousands of design options in the time it takes a human architect to draft a single sketch.

Humor:

Imagine an AI suggesting a building design that looks like a giant seashell, and the architect responds, "That's great, but I'm not sure it'll fit in downtown New York."

Future Vision:

In the future, AI could become a standard tool in creative industries. AI-Designed Fashion Collections: In fashion, designers will use AI to predict future trends and generate entire clothing lines based on emerging consumer preferences. These systems will not just follow trends but shape them, suggesting bold, new aesthetics that blend cultural insights and sustainability practices.

Chapter 3
Human Signal

Human thought and emotional intelligence are at the heart of what makes us truly human. Our minds have the incredible ability to understand and manage complicated emotions, notice subtle social signals, and empathize with others in ways that no other species—or even machines—can match. Our ability to not only process information but to weave it into a broader tapestry of emotional insight, personal experiences, and moral reflection is what truly sets us apart.

Human emotional intelligence (EQ) is a powerful force. It's the capacity to perceive, interpret, and manage emotions—both our own and those of others—allowing us to navigate the world in deeply meaningful ways. While cognitive intelligence (IQ) provides the logic and reasoning necessary for decision-making, it is EQ that gives decisions depth and humanity. EQ allows us to read between the lines, to understand the unspoken cues in a conversation, and to connect with people on an emotional level. This ability to feel, empathize, and intuit is not just a skill—it's a superpower that defines human interaction and drives our relationships, creativity, and empathy.

What makes human thinking truly special is its complexity and depth. It isn't just about processing information or solving problems in a mechanical way.

Our thoughts come from our life experiences, our understanding of the world around us, and our own personal perspectives. When we face a challenge, we don't just rely on cold, hard facts. We think about how our choices will affect our relationships, our well-being, and even our moral beliefs. We think beyond just success or failure. We engage with abstract concepts like justice, compassion, and integrity—concepts that can't be easily quantified or computed by machines.

For example, imagine you're in a leadership role tasked with making a difficult decision about downsizing a team. An AI system may crunch the numbers and suggest an optimal solution based on cost savings or efficiency. However, a human leader considers more than just the numbers. They think about the emotional impact on the team, the personal struggles of those who may be affected, and how the decision aligns with the company's values and long-term morale. It's this blending of logic with empathy that leads to decisions that honor both practical needs and human dignity.

Machines, no matter how sophisticated, lack this emotional depth. While AI can simulate empathy through learned behaviors and patterns, it does not genuinely feel or understand the human experience. It can recognize patterns of sadness or happiness, but it doesn't feel the weight of a difficult goodbye or the warmth of a comforting embrace. The nuances of joy, grief, fear, or love are beyond its capabilities, making the human experience irreplaceable in many realms of decision-making—particularly when moral or ethical dilemmas arise. This difference is crucial. It reminds us that, even as technology continues to grow, human beings will always have a unique and important role in making decisions, especially when it comes to complex social situations or ethical issues that require more than just logic.

As we continue to integrate AI into more aspects of our lives, the uniqueness of human thought will only become more apparent. Machines can assist us in many ways, helping us to be more efficient, more informed, and even more creative, but they cannot replicate the full depth of human understanding. Our emotions, experiences, and values form a unique "signal" that makes us human. This signal is not something that can be programmed or reduced to code—it's the essence of our humanity, and it will always be central to how we navigate the world and make decisions.

Real-Life Example: Emotional Intelligence in Leadership

Human beings are more than logical problem-solvers; we have emotional intelligence (EI), which allows us to perceive, manage, and respond to emotions in ourselves and others. Think about great leaders like **Jacinda Ardern** or **Satya Nadella**. Their success stems not just from their strategic skills, but from their ability to understand and connect emotionally with others. Nadella, for instance, transformed Microsoft by fostering a culture of empathy, encouraging open dialogue, and focusing on employee well-being.

Why It Matters: Emotional intelligence in leadership demonstrates how empathy and human connection drive organizational success. Leaders show that prioritizing emotional understanding fosters trust, collaboration, and innovation. This matters to everyone because workplaces that emphasize EI create environments where individuals feel valued, enabling personal growth and collective progress. It's a reminder that effective leadership goes beyond strategy—it's about truly connecting with people.

Reference –

- **Example of Satya Nadella:** Referenced from his leadership at Microsoft as documented in multiple business journals and interviews.

- **Jacinda Ardern's Leadership:** Public speeches and interviews have highlighted her empathy-driven approach during crises like the Christchurch shooting.

Analogy

If human intelligence is like a computer, then emotional intelligence is the software upgrade that helps you not only process data but also understand *why* people act the way they do. Imagine AI systems as robots following direct commands—without emotional intelligence, they might solve problems, but they wouldn't know how to respond when someone is upset or anxious.

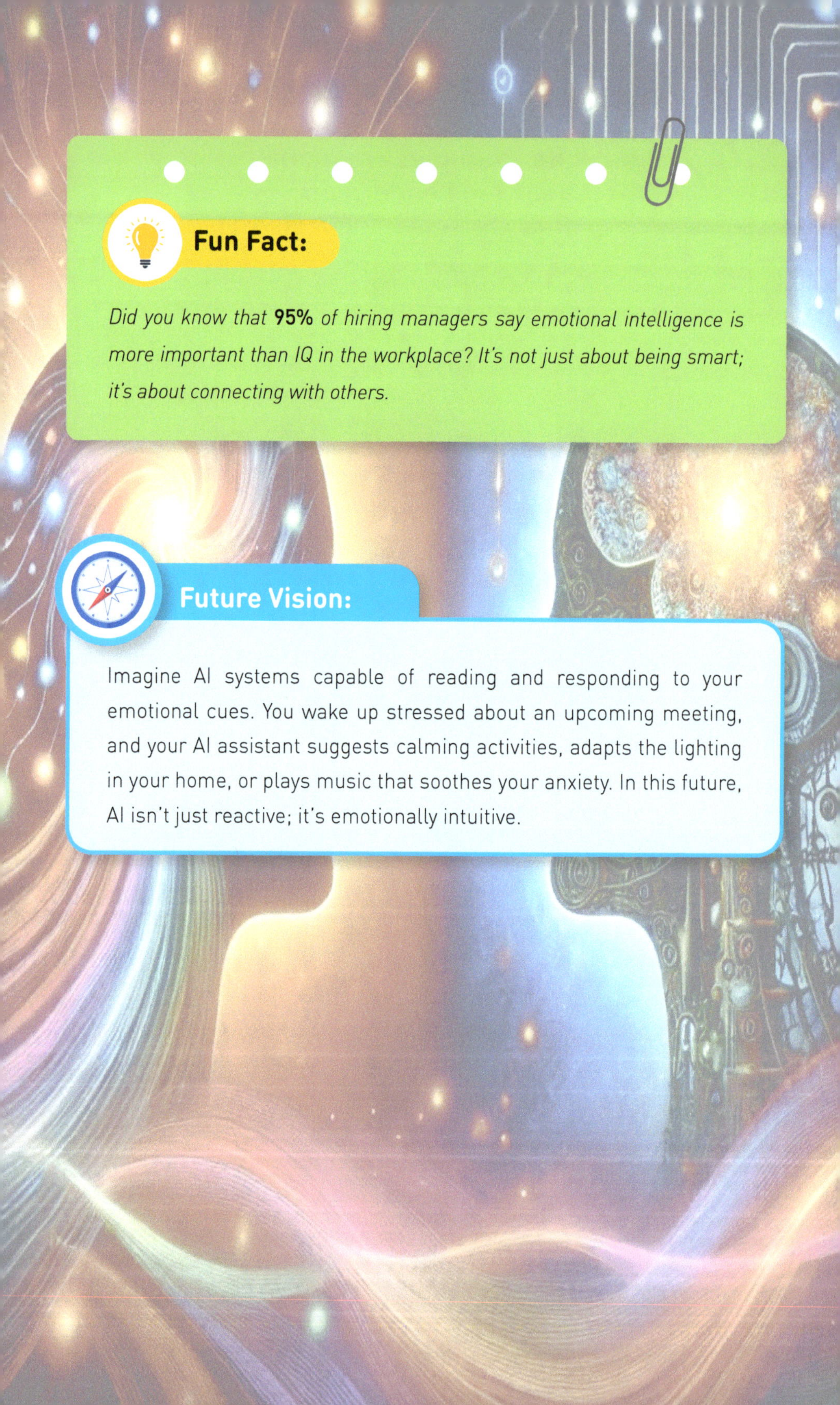

Fun Fact:

Did you know that **95%** of hiring managers say emotional intelligence is more important than IQ in the workplace? It's not just about being smart; it's about connecting with others.

Future Vision:

Imagine AI systems capable of reading and responding to your emotional cues. You wake up stressed about an upcoming meeting, and your AI assistant suggests calming activities, adapts the lighting in your home, or plays music that soothes your anxiety. In this future, AI isn't just reactive; it's emotionally intuitive.

3.2   Decoding the Complexity of Human Perception and Decision-Making

The way humans perceive the world and make decisions is incredibly complex, yet somehow it feels effortless. Every moment, we're flooded with sensory information—what we see, hear, feel, and even what we intuit without consciously realizing it. And from all this input, we manage to focus on what matters most. But we don't just process facts like a machine would. Instead, we weave them through a personal filter made up of our experiences, emotions, cultural backgrounds, and the long-term impacts of our choices. It's this rich tapestry of perception that allows us to engage with the world in ways that feel deeply human.

Human perception is subjective by nature, which is what makes each of us unique. Two people can experience the exact same event and walk away with completely different interpretations. Our perceptions are colored by our individual stories—our personal histories, the emotions we attach to certain situations, and even the mental shortcuts or biases we've picked up over time. For instance, someone who has faced failure might approach a new challenge with caution, while someone who's enjoyed a string of successes may dive in fearlessly. These differences show just how layered human perception is; it's not just about the facts but how we relate to them.

Making decisions isn't just a cold, logical exercise for us. Sure, we analyze data and weigh the pros and cons, but we also factor in how decisions will make us feel, how they might impact others, and whether they align with our values. Take, for example, the decision to change careers. On paper, a new job might offer better pay and more benefits, but your emotional ties to your current role—the friendships you've built or the sense of purpose you feel—will likely play just as big a role in your decision-making process. It's this balance between logic and emotion that makes human decision-making so intricate and, in many ways, so powerful.

For artificial intelligence, trying to replicate this kind of human complexity is an enormous task. While machine learning systems can be trained on massive amounts of data to imitate how we make decisions, they don't truly understand context or the subtle details that humans naturally grasp. Humans often use intuition—quick, almost instinctive decision-making based on a deep well of subconscious knowledge. In contrast, AI relies on pre-set rules and formulas, and it can't easily match the flexibility or creativity that humans bring to the table.

In many ways, the human approach to decision-making is something to be celebrated, not overshadowed by AI. Our unique ability to balance facts with feelings, to understand both the data and the emotional landscape of a situation, gives us an edge that machines simply don't have. Even as AI becomes more integrated into our daily lives, it's clear that the human touch—our ability to navigate complexity with both logic and empathy—will always play a vital role in decision-making.

This difference leads to an important question: can machines ever really think like humans? While AI is incredibly effective in areas where logic and data are the key drivers—like diagnosing diseases or organizing supply chains—it struggles with things like uncertainty, ambiguity, and the emotional layers that often shape human decisions. These qualities are the very core of human decision-making, and they're hard to teach a machine.

When making decisions, are we purely logical beings? Far from it. We weigh pros and cons, but we also listen to our hearts—considering how a choice feels, how it impacts others, and whether it aligns with our values. Imagine choosing a new job. Do you focus only on salary and benefits? Or do emotional ties, friendships, and purpose tip the scale? This balance between logic and emotion is what makes human decision-making powerful yet nuanced. So, as AI grows in capability, where does that leave us? Perhaps it's not about competition but collaboration. Let machines handle the data overload while humans focus on creativity, empathy, and critical thinking. Together, we can forge a future where human intuition and artificial intelligence thrive side by side. Isn't that the ultimate partnership?

Real-Life Example: Cognitive Bias in Decision-Making

Humans don't always make decisions based on logic or facts. **Cognitive biases**—like the *confirmation bias* (favoring information that supports our beliefs) or *recency bias* (placing more weight on recent information)—influence how we perceive the world and make choices. For instance, a doctor may diagnose an illness based on symptoms they've seen recently, even if a rarer condition fits the symptoms better. This makes human decision-making incredibly nuanced and sometimes unpredictable.

Analogy

Our brains are like filters. Every piece of information we encounter gets filtered through our experiences, emotions, and biases. Think of a camera lens—two people using the same camera might take completely different photos based on how they focus the lens. Similarly, two people may perceive the same event differently based on their cognitive "lenses."

Why It Matters: Understanding cognitive biases highlights how human decision-making is shaped by perceptions rather than pure logic. This matters because these biases can impact critical areas like healthcare, justice, and business. Recognizing and addressing these biases can lead to fairer, more accurate decisions, benefiting everyone by reducing errors and fostering better outcomes in both personal and professional spheres.

References

Daniel Kahneman's Research on Decision-Making: His book *Thinking, Fast and Slow* explains how biases influence decisions, which can be found through public sources and interviews.

Storytelling:

Take the example of **Daniel Kahneman's** research on decision-making. He showed that even highly trained experts can make irrational decisions due to cognitive biases. In his studies, doctors, lawyers, and judges—people we rely on for critical thinking—were influenced by subconscious biases in their judgments.

Interactive Thought:

Think about the last time you made a major decision. Did you consider all the facts, or were you influenced by what you *wanted* to believe? Now imagine how AI might have assisted you in making a more objective decision.

Future Vision:

In the future, AI systems could act as co-pilots in decision-making, helping us identify when our biases are affecting our choices. For example, before making a major financial investment, your AI assistant might remind you of historical patterns or cognitive biases you might be falling prey to, helping you make more informed, unbiased decisions.

3.3   Translating Human Values into Machine Learning Models

One of the most intriguing challenges in the world of artificial intelligence (AI) is how to embed human values into machine learning models in a way that makes sense to both humans and machines. AI systems are amazing at sifting through vast amounts of data and recognizing patterns, but they don't inherently "know" the deeper, often abstract concepts that guide human behavior—things like morality, fairness, and justice. These are the core values that shape our decisions and interactions and ensuring that AI aligns with them is not just a technical issue, but an ethical one.

At first glance, it might seem straightforward: teach a machine the rules of morality, and problem solved. But the reality is far more complex. Human values aren't hardwired or universal; they are shaped by personal experiences, societal norms, and cultural context. What's considered ethical or fair in one part of the world may be viewed very differently elsewhere. Take, for instance, the concept of fairness. In some societies, fairness is about treating everyone the same, while in others, fairness means offering extra support to those who are disadvantaged. This makes it incredibly difficult to develop a one-size-fits-all approach to embedding values in AI systems.

Then, there's the issue of bias, which complicates things even further. AI models are trained on historical data, and that data often contains the biases of the societies that generated it. If we're not careful, these models can absorb and even amplify those biases, perpetuating the very inequalities we're trying to avoid. For instance, if an AI system is trained on biased hiring data, it may inadvertently favor candidates from certain demographics while disadvantaging others, without ever being explicitly programmed to do so. This makes the stakes incredibly high: if we don't get this right, AI could reinforce harmful practices, instead of helping us move beyond them.

So, how do we make sure AI systems uphold human values? The answer lies not just in technology, but in collaboration. Designing ethical AI requires more than just data scientists and engineers; it demands the input of ethicists, sociologists, legal experts, and community leaders. This interdisciplinary approach ensures that we're not just building systems that "work," but ones that work for everyone. It's about asking deeper questions: Who benefits from this technology? Who might be harmed? What unintended consequences could arise? These questions don't have simple answers, but grappling with them is essential if we want AI to be a force for good.

For example, consider the growing use of AI in criminal justice systems. Algorithms are increasingly being used to predict whether individuals are likely to reoffend, and these predictions can influence decisions about bail, sentencing, and parole. While AI can process data far faster than any human could, it's crucial to remember that this data is based on past criminal justice practices, which may have been influenced by systemic biases. If an AI system isn't carefully designed to account for these biases, it could end up perpetuating them, leading to unfair outcomes for certain groups of people. By involving ethicists and legal scholars in the design process, developers can work to ensure that the AI takes into account broader questions of justice and fairness.

Another promising approach to embedding human values into AI is through transparency and accountability. AI systems should not operate as "black boxes" where decisions are made without any clear understanding of how or why they were reached. Instead, we need systems that are explainable, where people can understand the reasoning behind the AI's conclusions. This fosters trust and allows for meaningful oversight. If an AI makes a decision that seems unfair or biased, there should be a way to trace that decision back through the data and algorithms to identify where things went wrong. This kind of transparency is essential for ensuring that AI systems can be corrected when they fall short of our ethical expectations.

Ultimately, translating human values into machine learning models is about more than just preventing harm—it's about building a future where AI helps to enhance human well-being, justice, and equality. It's a future where technology not only reflects the best of who we are but also pushes us to be better, to challenge our biases, and to expand our definitions of fairness and morality. While the road ahead is complex, the promise of AI—when guided by human values—offers incredible potential for positive transformation. But that transformation will only happen if we're willing to engage deeply, think critically, and design ethically from the very beginning.

In essence, embedding human values in AI isn't just about making machines more human-like—it's about making sure that, as AI continues to shape our world, it does so in a way that is aligned with the diverse and evolving values of humanity itself.

Real-Life Example: Google's AI Ethics Board

The challenge of teaching machines to understand and act on human values is monumental. In 2019, **Google** created an AI ethics board to guide its decision-making around AI, particularly when it comes to sensitive issues like facial recognition and autonomous weapons. The goal was to ensure that AI systems don't just optimize for efficiency but also align with human values like fairness, transparency, and accountability. However, the board faced intense criticism and was disbanded just a week after its formation, showing how difficult it is to balance technological progress with human values.

Why It Matters: The rise and fall of Google's AI ethics board underscores the immense challenge of aligning AI advancements with human values. This matters because unchecked AI development could lead to ethical dilemmas affecting privacy, fairness, and accountability. It highlights the urgent need for transparent, inclusive frameworks to guide technology in ways that prioritize societal well-being over mere efficiency.

Analogy ?

Translating human values into machine learning is like trying to teach a robot to cook based on your family's secret recipes. It can follow the instructions, but it doesn't know why certain ingredients are important or how a dish makes people feel. Just like with AI, the challenge lies in embedding values that are deeply human and often hard to define.

Reference: This incident is documented in public news articles from 2019. Google created an AI ethics board but it was quickly dissolved, covered by sources such as *The Verge* and *Wired*.

Storytelling:

Imagine designing an AI that evaluates job applications. If this AI is trained only on historical data, it might reinforce biases like favoring male candidates over female ones. The challenge for developers is to embed values like *equality* and *diversity* into the AI, ensuring it doesn't perpetuate past injustices.

Fun Fact:

Did you know that AI systems trained on biased data can make biased decisions? In 2018, Amazon had to scrap its AI hiring tool because it was discriminating against female candidates.

Future Vision:

Imagine a future where AI systems are capable of learning and adapting to societal shifts in values. As global conversations about fairness, sustainability, and ethics evolve, AI would update its algorithms to reflect these new norms, ensuring that machine learning models remain aligned with current human values.

3.4   Ethical Considerations of Interpreting the Human Signal

As artificial intelligence (AI) and machine learning continue to evolve, they offer exciting possibilities for understanding and predicting human behavior. Whether it's AI interpreting emotions through facial recognition, analyzing voice patterns, or predicting actions based on behavior models, these technologies are poised to change how we interact with machines and each other. But with this innovation comes a complex web of ethical concerns that we can't afford to overlook. In fact, the more AI tries to read and react to human signals, the greater the need for careful thought about issues like privacy, consent, fairness, and accountability.

Let's start with one of the biggest ethical questions: **how well can AI really interpret human signals?** Human emotions and behaviors are incredibly nuanced, influenced by a multitude of factors, such as culture, context, and personal experience. When AI systems attempt to read emotions through a smile, a frown, or a particular tone of voice, they are essentially reducing these complex human experiences into data points. The risk here is oversimplification. A person might be smiling out of nervousness, but the AI might interpret it as happiness. Similarly, emotions like frustration, confusion, or excitement can manifest in subtle ways that are easy for machines to misinterpret. When these mistakes happen, they can lead to harmful consequences—especially when AI is used in critical areas like law enforcement, healthcare, or job recruitment.

Take facial recognition technology, for instance. It's used in everything from security systems to unlocking smartphones, but its application in more sensitive areas—like policing or public surveillance—raises significant privacy and ethical concerns. If an AI system misidentifies someone based on facial data, it could lead to wrongful arrests or worse. The potential for bias is another serious concern. If AI is trained on flawed or incomplete datasets that reflect historical inequalities, it could end up reinforcing those same biases. For example, an AI system used in hiring might unconsciously favor candidates who fit a particular profile that has been historically successful, while unfairly filtering out those who don't fit the mold, even if they're equally qualified.

The problem doesn't just stop with misinterpretation. **Transparency** is another key issue. AI systems, especially complex ones based on deep learning, often operate like black boxes, where the inner workings and decision-making processes are opaque, even to their developers. How does an AI decide which job candidate is the best fit? How does it flag someone as a security risk based on body language? If the logic behind these decisions isn't clear or explainable, it's easy for people to lose trust in the system. Worse, it can lead to situations where decisions are made that impact lives, and no one can fully explain why or how those decisions were reached. In healthcare, for instance, if an AI recommends one treatment plan over another, doctors and patients need to understand the reasoning to make informed decisions. A lack of transparency can lead to mistrust, hesitation, and even legal complications.

Privacy is perhaps one of the most pressing ethical concerns in the age of AI. As systems become more capable of interpreting human signals like facial expressions or body language, the question arises: how much of our personal data is being collected, and how is it being used? Most people are unaware of how much of their behavior is being tracked, whether it's online browsing habits, social media interactions, or even biometric data like fingerprints and facial scans. There's a growing unease around how this data is being used to predict and influence behavior, often without clear consent. Imagine walking into a store and having an AI system analyze your facial expression to predict your mood and tailor its marketing strategy accordingly. It might sound convenient, but it raises serious questions about personal autonomy and consent. Shouldn't people have the right to choose how their data is used or if it's used at all?

Bias is another thorny issue. AI learns from historical data, and if that data is biased, the AI will be too. This could have serious implications in areas like hiring, law enforcement, and even social services. For instance, if an AI system used in hiring decisions has been trained on data that reflects gender or racial biases, it might favor certain groups over others, perpetuating inequality. In policing, AI used to predict criminal behavior could disproportionately target minority communities if it's based on biased historical data. These biases aren't always easy to spot, making it crucial for developers to be vigilant and proactive in ensuring that AI systems are as fair and unbiased as possible.

Finally, **regulation and policy** will play an increasingly important role in governing the ethical use of AI. Governments and regulatory bodies need to step in to set guidelines for the responsible use of AI, particularly when it comes to sensitive areas like privacy, bias, and transparency. Clear laws and standards will help ensure that AI is used in a way that protects individuals' rights and prevents harm.

Transparency adds another layer of complexity. How can we trust a system whose decision-making is a "black box," even to its creators? If an AI flags someone as a security risk or recommends a medical treatment, shouldn't we know why? Without clear reasoning, trust erodes, and accountability becomes murky.

So, where do we draw the line? Can regulation keep up with AI's rapid evolution? Governments and policymakers must step in to set standards, ensuring fairness, transparency, and respect for individual rights. As AI grows, its ethical use depends not just on technology but on the values we choose to embed in it.

Ultimately, the real question is: What kind of future do we want to create? One where AI complements humanity or one where it complicates it? The answer lies in balancing innovation with integrity, safeguarding both progress and our shared humanity.

In summary, the ethical considerations surrounding AI's interpretation of human signals are vast and complex, but they are also critical. As AI continues to evolve, the choices we make today will shape how these systems impact society tomorrow. By prioritizing fairness, transparency, accountability, and privacy, we can help ensure that AI enhances human life rather than complicates it. The future of AI isn't just about technology—it's about values, trust, and the kind of world we want to create.

Real-Life Example: Facebook's Data Scandal

The interpretation of human data brings significant ethical challenges. One high-profile example is **Facebook's data scandal** involving Cambridge Analytica. Personal data from millions of Facebook users was harvested without their consent and used to influence political campaigns. This raised serious concerns about privacy, data security, and how AI algorithms interpret and manipulate human behavior.

Why It Matters: Facebook's data scandal reveals the critical risks of unchecked data collection and misuse. This matters because it highlights how personal data, if exploited, can undermine privacy, manipulate public opinion, and threaten democracy. It underscores the urgent need for stronger regulations, transparency, and accountability to protect individuals in the digital age.

References - **Cambridge Analytica Scandal**: Widely reported in media outlets such as *The Guardian* and *The New York Times*, detailing the ethical breaches around data privacy.

Analogy

Imagine someone listening to a conversation between two people, then using that information to manipulate one of them without their knowledge. This is what happens when AI systems gather and use data without transparent consent. It's not just about collecting data; it's about how that data is used to influence decisions and behaviors in subtle ways.

Thought-Provoking Question:

What if AI could predict your next action based on your online activity? Would you feel comfortable if an algorithm knew when you were most likely to buy something or vote for a particular candidate?

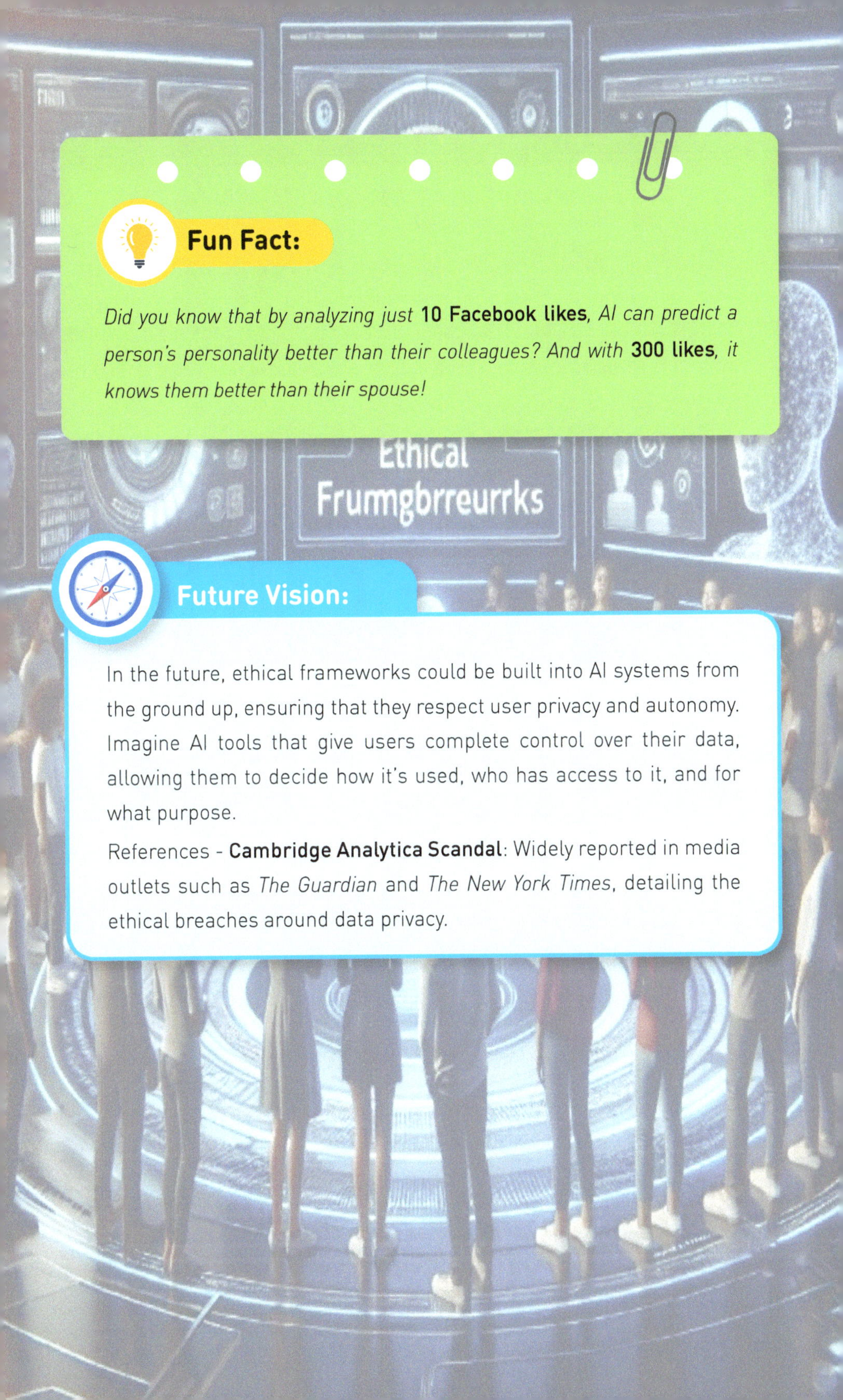

Fun Fact:

*Did you know that by analyzing just **10 Facebook likes**, AI can predict a person's personality better than their colleagues? And with **300 likes**, it knows them better than their spouse!*

Future Vision:

In the future, ethical frameworks could be built into AI systems from the ground up, ensuring that they respect user privacy and autonomy. Imagine AI tools that give users complete control over their data, allowing them to decide how it's used, who has access to it, and for what purpose.

References - **Cambridge Analytica Scandal**: Widely reported in media outlets such as *The Guardian* and *The New York Times*, detailing the ethical breaches around data privacy.

3.5 How AI Learns to Respond to Human Behaviors and Needs

Despite some challenges, AI is getting better at learning how to respond to human behaviors and needs. Using techniques like reinforcement learning, natural language processing, and sentiment analysis, AI systems can be trained to understand a variety of human inputs. For instance, in customer service, AI-powered chatbots can chat with users in a way that feels natural, providing personalized responses based on past interactions and what the user likes.

But it doesn't stop there! One of the most exciting aspects of AI is its **adaptability**. As these systems gather more information over time, they continuously refine their responses. Imagine a recommendation engine like the ones used by streaming platforms such as Netflix or Spotify. These AI systems learn from your viewing and listening habits, adjusting their suggestions to align with your unique tastes. The more you engage, the better they become at predicting what you might want to enjoy next, creating a tailored experience that feels almost intuitive.

However, it's important to remember that while AI can spot patterns in how people behave, it doesn't truly "understand" human needs. Its responses are based on data and algorithms, not on real empathy or comprehension. This distinction is important because it underscores the necessity of a human touch in situations that demand emotional intelligence, ethical decision-making, or a nuanced understanding of personal relationships.

This distinction is important because it underscores the necessity of a human touch in situations that demand emotional intelligence, ethical decision-making, or a nuanced understanding of personal relationships.

For example, consider a scenario where someone is navigating a difficult emotional experience. An AI may be able to analyze the data surrounding that person's behavior, but it cannot offer the depth of understanding or comfort that a human friend or counselor can provide. In moments that require compassion or moral judgment, AI falls short.

Ultimately, while AI is rapidly improving its ability to interpret and respond to human signals, it cannot replicate the rich and intricate ways in which we engage with the world. AI can help us process information more efficiently and assist in solving problems, but it's our emotions, values, and perceptions—those uniquely human qualities—that truly shape our experiences. As we continue to harness the power of AI, it's essential to remember that technology is a tool meant to enhance our human experience, not replace it. The essence of humanity remains irreplaceable, and our ability to connect with one another on a deeper level is what truly defines and but the essence of what makes us human—our emotions, values, and perceptions—remains unique to us.

Does AI actually "understand" us? While it excels at identifying patterns in data and predicting preferences, its knowledge is algorithmic, not empathetic. For instance, a chatbot can tailor responses to your mood based on past interactions, but it doesn't *feel* your emotions or grasp the depth of your needs. Could it offer solace during a personal crisis or understand the nuance of a moral dilemma? Not quite—these are realms where human intuition and emotional intelligence remain unmatched.

What does this mean for the balance between AI and humanity? Should we trust AI to handle sensitive roles that demand compassion or ethical reasoning? Perhaps the key is recognizing AI as a tool—powerful, transformative, yet incomplete without human oversight and emotional depth.

As we innovate, the challenge is clear: How do we ensure AI enhances our lives without overshadowing the very qualities that make us human? By keeping people at the center of this technological journey, we can create a future where AI complements our humanity rather than competes with it.

Real-Life Example: Personalized AI Assistants like Siri and Alexa

AI is already learning to respond to human behaviors through systems like **Siri**, **Alexa**, and **Google Assistant**. These tools learn from our interactions, becoming more personalized the more we use them. If you frequently ask Siri for weather updates, it will start offering that information without being prompted. AI systems are also being used in healthcare to track patient behaviors, adjusting treatment plans based on individual needs.

Why It Matters: This fusion of personalized AI assistants and healthcare systems exemplifies how machine learning is transforming everyday life. AI is no longer a static tool—it's becoming a dynamic partner in our daily routines and in critical areas like health. These systems have the potential to improve efficiency, enhance user experience, and even save lives by offering tailored recommendations based on real-time data. As AI systems continue to learn and adapt, their ability to serve us becomes more intuitive, providing a level of personalization that was once thought to be out of reach.

Analogy

Imagine having a personal assistant who learns from everything you do—what time you wake up, your favorite breakfast, and even how you prefer your coffee. Over time, this assistant doesn't just follow orders; it anticipates your needs. That's exactly how AI assistants are evolving.

Reference: Numerous case studies and articles about how AI learns from user behavior can be found in tech journals and publications like *MIT Technology Review* and *Wired*.

Humor:

If you ask Alexa to tell you a joke, you'll probably get a cheesy response. But over time, as AI systems get better at reading human behaviors, don't be surprised if Alexa starts telling jokes that are tailored to your specific sense of humor!

Fun Fact:

*Did you know that **50%** of all internet searches are expected to be voice searches by 2025? AI assistants are becoming such a part of our daily lives that we may soon be talking to them more than typing.*

Future Vision:

Imagine a future where AI systems not only respond to your requests but also anticipate them without you defining and setting for AI. You're driving home after a long day, and your AI knows to dim the lights, adjust the thermostat, and order your favorite takeout—all without you lifting a finger. These systems could evolve to understand your emotional state, offering support when you're stressed or suggesting activities when you need a break.

Human and fusion systems
Dynamic, AI systems
and self-optimizing systems
Real-time adaptive AI
Agile productives
real-rah-time
adractive tools

Chapter **4**
Adaptive Nexus

4.1 The Fluid Relationship Between Humans and Adaptive AI

The relationship between humans and artificial intelligence (AI) has undergone a major shift over recent years. We used to think of AI as a rigid system, limited to performing tasks based on pre-programmed rules. But as AI has evolved, it's become clear that it's much more flexible than we initially thought. AI is now capable of learning and adapting in real time, evolving based on the information it gathers. This ability has opened the door to a new kind of partnership between humans and machines, one that is much more collaborative and personalized.

At the heart of this transformation is the concept of adaptability. AI no longer functions as a static tool; instead, it learns from its interactions with humans, gradually fine-tuning its responses to become more helpful and intuitive over time. This adaptability makes AI systems more personalized, creating a tailored experience for each user. The more we engage with AI, the more it adjusts to our habits and preferences, and in turn, the more useful and integrated it becomes in our daily lives.

This shift in how we perceive AI has far-reaching implications. As the technology becomes more adaptable, it starts to feel less like a distant, cold machine and more like an active partner in our lives. The more personalized AI becomes, the more it integrates into our routines, helping us manage tasks, make decisions, and solve problems. It moves from being a simple tool we use to an active participant in our workflow, understanding and responding to our needs in a more dynamic way.

One of the most important aspects of this evolving relationship is trust. As humans, we tend to rely on systems that we understand and feel comfortable with. As AI becomes more adaptive, it naturally builds a sense of trust by demonstrating its ability to learn and improve based on our interactions. When we see AI making our lives easier and more efficient, we become more comfortable relying on it for more complex tasks. Over time, this trust deepens, and AI shifts from being something we use to something we rely on.

The concept of trust is particularly important in fields like healthcare or critical decision-making, where the stakes are high. In these environments, AI's ability to learn and adapt in real time can make all the difference. Doctors, for instance, might rely on AI systems to help analyze patient data and offer treatment suggestions. As they witness the accuracy and reliability of these systems, their confidence in AI grows. Eventually, AI becomes an essential partner in the decision-making process, one that doctors trust to provide valuable insights they might not have the time or capacity to uncover on their own.

This growing trust between humans and AI is paving the way for a more symbiotic relationship. AI doesn't just perform tasks for us—it learns from us, adapts to our needs, and grows alongside us. As we continue to interact with AI, the technology becomes more capable of anticipating our needs and offering more relevant solutions. This creates a feedback loop in which humans and AI work together more effectively over time, each enhancing the other's abilities.

The relationship between humans and adaptive AI also has profound implications for the future of work. As AI becomes more capable of learning and adjusting to human behavior, it will play a larger role in decision-making processes across a range of industries. In business, for example, adaptive AI could help managers make more informed decisions by analyzing data and offering insights that would take a human much longer to process. This allows companies to operate more efficiently and respond more quickly to changes in the market.

In creative industries, adaptive AI could help spark new ideas by offering suggestions and generating concepts based on patterns it has learned from past interactions. This kind of collaboration between human creativity and AI's analytical capabilities has the potential to unlock entirely new forms of expression and innovation. The more fluid and dynamic the relationship becomes, the more opportunities there will be to push the boundaries of what we can achieve.

However, with this deeper integration of AI into our lives comes the question of balance. As AI becomes more intelligent and capable, it's essential to ensure that humans remain in control of the decision-making process. While AI can offer valuable insights and suggestions, it's crucial that we maintain transparency and understanding of how these systems operate. Trusting AI doesn't mean handing over control entirely—it means leveraging AI as a partner while retaining human oversight and ethical considerations.

Ultimately, the fluid relationship between humans and adaptive AI is just the beginning of a larger transformation in how we interact with technology. As AI continues to evolve and learn, the line between human intelligence and machine intelligence will blur further, creating a more integrated and seamless experience. This collaboration has the potential to unlock new levels of productivity, creativity, and innovation, allowing us to achieve things that neither humans nor AI could accomplish alone.

Looking ahead, the partnership between humans and AI will only grow stronger. As the technology becomes more adaptive, it will continue to learn from our interactions, becoming even more personalized and capable over time. This will lead to a more intuitive, seamless integration of AI into our everyday lives, where humans and machines work together in harmony. The future of AI is one of continuous evolution, where both humans and machines benefit from each other's strengths, driving progress in ways we are just beginning to imagine.

Real-Life Example: Netflix's Recommendation System

Netflix's AI is like that friend who always knows the perfect movie or TV show to recommend—except this one never runs out of suggestions. It learns your preferences with every click, scroll, and watch, becoming so good at predicting what you'll enjoy that sometimes it feels like it knows you better than you know yourself. This recommendation system doesn't just rely on the movies you've watched but also factors in what others with similar tastes enjoy, making its suggestions feel eerily accurate.

Why It Matters: Netflix's recommendation system is more than just a tool for suggesting content—it's a game-changer in how we consume entertainment. By leveraging AI to personalize the viewing experience, Netflix ensures that each user gets a tailored entertainment journey, reducing the time spent searching and increasing the chances of discovering new favorites. This seamless, personalized approach is part of what makes Netflix so addictive—it feels like the service is always in tune with what you're in the mood for, and that level of personalization is powered by sophisticated AI.

Reference: You can explore more about Netflix's recommendation algorithms and the technology behind them in articles from tech journals and publications like Wired and MIT Technology Review.

Analogy

Imagine having a friend who's been with you for years, watching movies with you and learning what you like, but instead of just offering a suggestion when asked, they constantly offer the next great pick without you even having to think about it. The longer you hang out with them, the better they get at reading your mind. Netflix's AI acts as this friend, constantly learning and adapting its recommendations to fit your evolving tastes, making it a seamless part of your entertainment experience.

Fun Fact:

*Netflix once awarded a **$1 million prize** to a team of developers for improving its recommendation engine by 10%! They're serious about keeping your movie nights perfectly tailored.*

Humor:

Imagine if your fridge could do the same thing—"I see you're out of ice cream...again. I'll just order more for you, shall I?"

Future Vision:

Adaptive AI will evolve to anticipate more than just your taste in movies. In the future, smart homes could adjust room temperatures based on your preferences *before* you even realize you're too hot or cold. AI might also adapt your work schedule according to your mental and physical state, making everyday life feel almost magical.

4.2   How AI Systems Learn and Evolve Alongside Human Users

AI systems are designed to learn and improve from the data they receive. At their core, they use machine learning, which helps them analyze large amounts of information and spot patterns that might be too complex for people to notice. The more an AI system interacts with users, the better it becomes at adapting to their needs and providing more accurate, helpful results.

What makes AI different from many other technologies is that it doesn't stay the same. It evolves over time. As it processes more data, it becomes smarter and more effective. This happens because AI systems use algorithms that adjust and improve based on their experiences. Each interaction with a user provides new data for the system to learn from, making it more refined and efficient in the future.

AI systems don't just learn from individual users—they gather insights from many people. This means that when one person uses the system, the AI also learns from the experiences of others. This allows it to make more informed decisions, benefiting all users. It's a continuous loop where users provide data, and the AI uses that data to improve and make better predictions or suggestions over time.

The learning process doesn't just happen on one side. When people interact with AI systems, they also influence how the AI behaves. Feedback, whether direct or indirect, plays an important role in this process. If a user rejects a suggestion or provides negative feedback, the AI can adjust its settings to offer more relevant results in the future. On the other hand, if the feedback is positive, the AI strengthens its approach to continue offering similar suggestions. This back-and-forth interaction ensures that AI systems keep improving.

This learning process is not static; it's constantly evolving. AI systems are designed to adapt to the changing needs and preferences of users. As they gather more data, they become better at predicting what users want or need, making the experience more personalized and efficient. Over time, AI systems build trust with their users by providing more accurate and tailored responses, which encourages people to rely on them more.

The relationship between humans and AI is becoming more dynamic. Rather than being fixed tools, AI systems are now evolving alongside humans, learning and adjusting based on our actions and preferences. This close interaction allows AI to become a valuable partner in everyday tasks, helping us by processing information more quickly and making better decisions. The more we interact with these systems, the better they become at understanding our needs and assisting us in more meaningful ways.

Furthermore, AI systems are not limited to learning from user interactions alone. They can also integrate data from a variety of external sources, such as social media, sensor data, and other Internet of Things (IoT) devices. This broader data pool allows AI to develop a more comprehensive view of the world and human behavior, which in turn enhances its predictive capabilities. By understanding patterns across different domains—whether it's health, consumer behavior, or environmental factors—AI can offer insights and recommendations that are more holistic and informed by a wider spectrum of knowledge. As AI continues to process these diverse inputs, its ability to adapt and anticipate the needs of users becomes more refined, creating an increasingly symbiotic relationship between human and machine.

In conclusion, AI's ability to learn and evolve with human users is key to its growing usefulness. By continuously collecting data and responding to feedback, AI systems can refine their functions to stay relevant and meet the needs of users. This ongoing improvement ensures that AI becomes more efficient and aligned with human expectations, making it a valuable and adaptive tool in our daily lives.

Real-Life Example: Google's AI-Powered G Suite

Google's AI-powered G Suite is like having a *personal assistant* that not only organizes your tasks but also learns how you work, communicates with others, and adapts to your style over time. Take Gmail's Smart Reply, for example. It's a small feature, but incredibly powerful—it analyzes the way you write and begins to offer email replies that feel like something you would say. As you interact with it more, Smart Reply becomes increasingly attuned to your tone, choice of words, and even your unique conversational habits. It's not just a tool; it's a collaborator, evolving with you to streamline communication and make your workday a little easier.

Why It Matters: Google's AI-powered G Suite is not just a productivity tool; it's a key to working smarter, not harder. The ability to personalize tasks, such as email responses, document drafting, and meeting scheduling, creates a frictionless workflow. Instead of spending time on repetitive actions like drafting a basic email or searching for a document, the AI does much of the heavy lifting, allowing users to focus on more critical tasks. The deeper the AI integrates into your work habits, the more it anticipates your needs, enabling you to accomplish more in less time. This level of automation and intelligence is a game-changer for both individuals and businesses looking to maximize productivity and efficiency.

Analogy

Imagine a friend who knows your communication style so well that they can finish your sentences for you. But instead of being annoying, they actually save you time by understanding your tone, preferences, and the context of your conversations. That's what Gmail's Smart Reply does—it becomes so aligned with your way of communicating that it feels almost like the AI is reading your mind. The more you use it, the more it begins to "speak your language" naturally.

Source: *Google AI Blog:* URL: https://ai.googleblog.com/

Fun Fact:

Gmail's **Smart Compose** *was trained on thousands of emails to learn how to craft human-like responses. It has learned so much that it can even insert humor into messages...okay, maybe not funny humor yet, but it's learning!*

Humor:

Imagine if Smart Compose gets too smart: "Hey boss, I'd love to take on that extra project!" Yeah, maybe tone it down, AI.

Future Vision:

Soon, AI systems might not just learn from us but from each other. Imagine your email AI talking to your task management AI, keeping your calendar updated, prioritizing your work, and ordering your coffee (decaf today, because it knows you were up late last night). And Imagine AI systems in classrooms evolving alongside students, identifying learning gaps and providing personalized content to address specific needs. As the student grows, so does the AI's ability to support them.

4.3   The Creation of Dynamic, Self-Optimizing Systems

One of the most significant developments in artificial intelligence is the rise of systems that can continuously improve themselves. These self-optimizing systems are designed to do more than just respond to inputs—they actively seek new ways to enhance their performance over time. Rather than being static, these systems evolve, learning from their interactions and experiences to become more effective in achieving their goals.

The key feature of these systems is their ability to gather new data on their own and use it to refine how they operate. They don't wait for human direction to make improvements but instead analyze the information they collect to find areas where they can optimize. This continuous learning process allows them to become more efficient, performing tasks more quickly and accurately with each iteration.

What makes these systems stand out is their independence. They are designed to function with minimal human input, automatically adjusting their behavior when needed. When something is not working as efficiently as it should, the system takes the initiative to correct it, ensuring that everything runs smoothly. This ability to adapt without constant supervision reduces the burden on humans while increasing overall productivity.

Moreover, the potential for these systems to integrate with others makes them even more powerful. When multiple systems work together, they can form a network that is constantly improving. This connected network allows for better coordination, as each system learns and adapts alongside the others, ensuring that processes are as streamlined and efficient as possible.

This adaptability is not limited to a specific task or function. These systems can be applied across different areas, continually evolving and improving as they are exposed to new data and challenges. Their flexibility makes them useful in a wide range of applications, offering a powerful tool for improving efficiency and performance in various settings.

In essence, the evolution of self-optimizing systems represents a major step forward in the development of artificial intelligence. These systems are not just reactive but proactive, continually learning and improving without the need for constant human intervention. Their ability to work independently and together with other systems opens up new possibilities for enhancing processes and achieving higher levels of efficiency. This ongoing evolution will likely play a crucial role in the future of technology, where machines are capable of learning and adapting on their own, continuously improving how they perform their functions.

Additionally, self-optimizing systems benefit from advancements in reinforcement learning, where they are able to refine their behavior through trial and error. This form of learning empowers the system to test various approaches, evaluate the results, and make adjustments accordingly. Over time, these systems accumulate a vast wealth of knowledge from their own experiences, allowing them to become increasingly precise and effective in achieving their goals. The more data they process, the more proficient they become in refining their processes, ultimately driving continuous innovation. With each iteration, these systems not only get better at what they do but also discover novel ways to achieve higher levels of optimization that were not previously considered.

In conclusion, these advanced systems are paving the way for a more autonomous future, where technology is not just a tool but an evolving partner that grows and improves through its experiences. The ability to self-optimize marks a shift towards more intelligent, adaptable systems that can enhance performance in ways that were previously unimaginable. This ongoing development promises to bring even greater efficiency and innovation as these systems continue to learn and evolve.

Real-Life Example: Tesla's Autopilot

Perfect example of how technology can continuously improve and adapt in real time. As Tesla cars rack up millions of miles on the road, the Autopilot system gathers data from every trip, fine-tuning its driving algorithms. A great example of this in action happened in 2021, when Tesla's Autopilot system became better at detecting emergency vehicles. This wasn't just because of new programming—it was the system learning from the experiences of millions of cars driving in real-world conditions. Each mile driven makes the system smarter and safer for all Tesla owners.

Why It Matters: This ability to self-optimize is what sets Tesla's Autopilot apart. It means that the system is never static—it's always evolving. Instead of relying solely on pre-programmed rules, it learns from each drive, constantly improving its responses and predictions. This helps make Tesla cars safer, smarter, and more efficient as they accumulate data. It's a huge step toward the future of autonomous vehicles, where every trip not only gets you to your destination but helps make the entire system more capable, reliable, and safer for everyone.

Reference: Tesla's technical papers and official updates on machine learning in autonomous driving systems (2021).

Analogy

Imagine Tesla's Autopilot as a new driver—one who starts off a bit unsure behind the wheel but gains more confidence and skill with every drive. Over time, this driver doesn't just learn from their own experiences but from the journeys of others as well. They start reacting better to pedestrians, sharp turns, or even those unexpected road hazards. Just like this driver, Tesla's system gets sharper, learning from every single car in the fleet, getting smarter with every new situation it encounters.

Fun Fact:

Elon Musk claims that **full self-driving cars** *could become a reality in the next few years. So, we might soon live in a world where cars need a software update instead of a tune-up.*

Humor:

"What do you mean I can't drive my car? It's updating!"—The future where your morning commute is delayed because your car is patching its latest AI firmware.

Future Vision:

Imagine a world where your entire life is self-optimizing, not just your car. AI systems could dynamically adjust your grocery lists, workout routines, and even your work schedule based on data it gathers about your habits. Without even you are telling AI to do.

4.4   Enhancing Productivity Through Real-Time Adaptive Tools

The rise of real-time adaptive tools powered by artificial intelligence has really changed how we work. These innovative tools can quickly respond to changing conditions, allowing us to make decisions faster and more effectively. In a world where things move quickly, having the ability to adapt can make a big difference in getting things done.

One of the biggest advantages of these AI-driven tools is their capability to analyze and interpret data as it comes in. Take project management software, for example. These systems can keep track of team dynamics and workload in real time. By continuously monitoring how tasks are progressing, the software can adjust deadlines or resource allocation as needed. This flexibility helps ensure that projects stay on track, even when unexpected challenges pop up.

Imagine a team racing against a tight deadline. The AI tool can monitor each member's progress and pinpoint any potential slowdowns. If someone is lagging behind, the system can suggest redistributing tasks to help balance the workload. This not only keeps the project moving forward but also alleviates pressure on any one person, contributing to a healthier, more supportive work environment.

The benefits of these real-time adaptive tools go beyond just project management; they can be applied in various fields to boost productivity. For instance, in finance, AI can analyze market trends as they happen, equipping traders with the insights they need to make informed decisions right on the spot. In an industry where timing is everything, this capability can be invaluable.

In the realm of education, adaptive learning platforms harness AI to tailor lessons to the individual needs and progress of each student. By closely analyzing how well students are doing, these systems can customize their learning experiences. This personalized approach makes it easier for students to grasp complex concepts and stay engaged in their studies, fostering a more effective learning environment.

The integration of real-time adaptive tools into our daily routines not only boosts productivity but also enhances job satisfaction. By alleviating some of the stress associated with tight deadlines and high-pressure decisions, these tools create a more manageable work experience. Team members can feel reassured knowing they have intelligent systems supporting them, ready to make quick adjustments as circumstances change.

As these tools continue to evolve, their potential for enhancing productivity will only grow. Ongoing advancements in AI will lead to even more sophisticated systems that can anticipate needs, streamline processes, and provide deeper insights. This continual improvement means that organizations can remain agile and competitive in a constantly changing environment.

As the capabilities of real-time adaptive tools expand, we also see a shift in how they empower individuals to take ownership of their tasks and performance. These tools don't just react to external data—they also provide users with real-time feedback, nudging them toward more effective choices. For example, AI in a productivity app could highlight patterns in a user's work habits, offering suggestions for optimizing workflows or time management.

In summary, real-time adaptive tools powered by AI are reshaping how we work by improving our ability to respond to dynamic situations. By analyzing data and offering actionable insights, these systems empower teams to make quicker, better decisions. This adaptability not only enhances productivity but also contributes to a more positive work atmosphere. As technology advances, these tools will play an even more vital role in our professional lives, helping us work more effectively and collaboratively.

Real-Life Example:
Microsoft's AI-Powered Office Suite

Microsoft's AI-powered Office Suite is transforming how we work every day. Imagine you're working on a spreadsheet in Excel, and it automatically suggests the perfect formula based on what you're trying to calculate. Or maybe you're creating a PowerPoint presentation, and the tool offers design suggestions that perfectly match your content. Even Word is getting smarter, helping with grammar, sentence structure, and even adjusting your writing tone. These aren't just helpful features—they learn from your behavior, evolving over time to offer even better, more personalized support as you work.

Why It Matters: What makes this so powerful is how these tools continuously improve based on your behavior. They aren't static—they evolve and grow alongside you, getting smarter the more you use them. This means that as you work on more projects and tasks, the tools become more aligned with your needs, streamlining your workflow and improving productivity. It's not just about making work easier in the moment—it's about making you more effective over time, with a set of tools that learns and adapts to your unique style.

Analogy

Think of Microsoft's AI-powered Office Suite as a personal assistant who gets to know you better the more you work together. At first, it may offer basic help, but as you continue using the tools, it begins to anticipate your needs, offering smarter suggestions. Just like a colleague who learns your preferences and workflow, the Office Suite adapts to how you work, making your tasks easier and more efficient with each use.

Reference: Microsoft's official updates on AI-powered Office tools and user personalization features (2021).

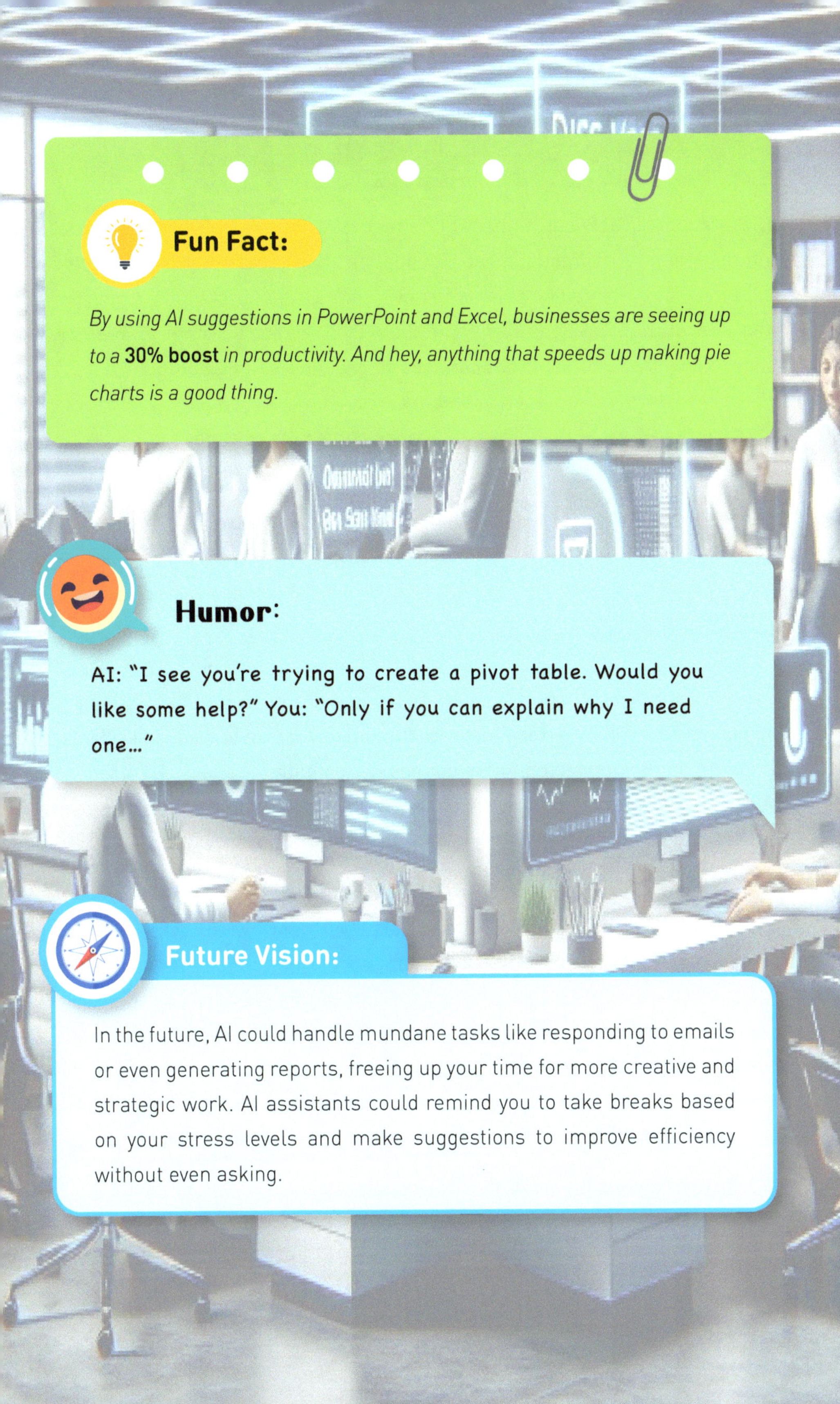

Fun Fact:

By using AI suggestions in PowerPoint and Excel, businesses are seeing up to a 30% boost in productivity. And hey, anything that speeds up making pie charts is a good thing.

Humor:

AI: "I see you're trying to create a pivot table. Would you like some help?" You: "Only if you can explain why I need one..."

Future Vision:

In the future, AI could handle mundane tasks like responding to emails or even generating reports, freeing up your time for more creative and strategic work. AI assistants could remind you to take breaks based on your stress levels and make suggestions to improve efficiency without even asking.

4.5   Interconnected Networks of AI and Human-Driven Innovation

The relationship between humans and adaptive AI goes beyond mere individual interactions; it represents the foundation for creating interconnected networks that propel innovation into new realms. As AI systems learn, grow, and evolve, they have the remarkable ability to connect with one another, sharing insights and data that can lead to groundbreaking solutions across various sectors. This synergy creates a dynamic ecosystem where both human creativity and machine intelligence contribute to enhanced problem-solving.

Take urban planning as an example. In our increasingly crowded cities, AI can analyze complex data sets, including traffic patterns, weather conditions, and public transport usage. By integrating information from different sources, AI can help city planners design smarter infrastructure that adapts to real-time circumstances. Imagine a city where traffic lights adjust their timings based on live traffic flow, public transport schedules are optimized for passenger demand, and streets are monitored for conditions that could lead to accidents. This kind of interconnected AI system has the potential to significantly reduce congestion, lower pollution levels, and ultimately enhance the quality of life for city residents.

Furthermore, this interconnectedness nurtures a collaborative spirit between humans and machines. As AI systems take over data-driven tasks—such as analyzing market trends, predicting customer behaviors, or optimizing resource allocation—humans are liberated to concentrate on areas where they truly excel: creative problem-solving, strategic planning, and empathetic decision-making. This shift in focus not only enhances efficiency but also allows for more meaningful contributions from individuals who can inject their unique perspectives and creativity into the process.

In a world where human-driven innovation flourishes alongside adaptive AI, we can envision a future rich in opportunities. For instance, industries such as healthcare, education, and environmental management could see profound transformations. Doctors might work alongside AI to develop personalized treatment plans by analyzing vast patient data, while educators could utilize AI to tailor learning experiences to the needs of individual students.

Moreover, the power of interconnected networks becomes particularly evident when diverse fields of human expertise converge with AI. In architecture, for instance, AI systems can process data about climate, structural integrity, and local materials, while architects bring their vision, artistic judgment, and contextual understanding of space. This creates a co-creative environment where AI enhances the precision and functionality of designs, while human ingenuity ensures that they are meaningful, aesthetically pleasing, and culturally relevant. Think about autonomous AI-driven robots working alongside conservationists to protect endangered species by tracking animal populations, analyzing habitats, and preventing poaching—bringing together technology and environmental stewardship in an unprecedented way.

Ultimately, the emergence of interconnected networks that harness the strengths of both humans and AI sets the stage for a collaborative future. By leveraging these synergies, we can address some of the most pressing challenges of our time, driving forward a new era of innovation that benefits everyone. The harmonious relationship between human ingenuity and adaptive AI will not only redefine industries but also reshape our society in ways we are just beginning to imagine.

Real-Life Example: AI-powered Tools For Disaster Response

The development of AI-powered tools for disaster response, like those used by the Red Cross, is a compelling example of human-driven innovation and AI working together. These AI systems are designed to analyze data from satellite images, social media feeds, and weather reports to predict areas that will need urgent help during natural disasters. In real time, they assist human teams by identifying disaster zones, tracking affected populations, and even mapping out areas for rescue operations. As these systems continue to gather data from past events, they become better at predicting and responding to future disasters, saving more lives and optimizing the resources of humanitarian organizations.

Why It Matters: This integration of AI into disaster response is a perfect example of how AI can augment human expertise to address global challenges. The AI doesn't replace human responders—it empowers them, helping to allocate resources more effectively, speed up decision-making, and ultimately save lives. The more data the system processes, the smarter it gets, improving the response to each new disaster. This evolving partnership between AI and human innovation demonstrates the tremendous potential of AI to not only enhance human efforts but also transform how we tackle urgent, real-world problems.

Analogy

Imagine an AI system as a *supercharged mapmaker* who helps rescue teams plan their missions. The mapmaker starts by using historical data to create a basic map of disaster-prone areas. Over time, as more data pours in from real-world events, the mapmaker adjusts and refines the map, learning how to better anticipate where help is needed most. The more disasters the system helps manage, the more precise and valuable its predictions become.

Reference: Red Cross and AI disaster response initiatives (2021)

Fun Fact:

GPT models have been used to write short stories, generate code, and even produce music! Who knew AI could help with your next big novel?

Humor:

One day, AI might win an Oscar for best original screenplay. "I'd like to thank the algorithms that made this possible..."

Future Vision:

We could be heading towards a world where interconnected AIs work together to create solutions for global problems. Imagine an AI-driven network connecting scientists, engineers, and entrepreneurs worldwide to tackle issues like climate change and poverty, all while learning from each other's breakthroughs. And Imagine a future where global networks of interconnected AI help solve complex problems like climate change. AI systems could analyze massive amounts of data in real-time, proposing innovative solutions that humans alone would struggle to find.

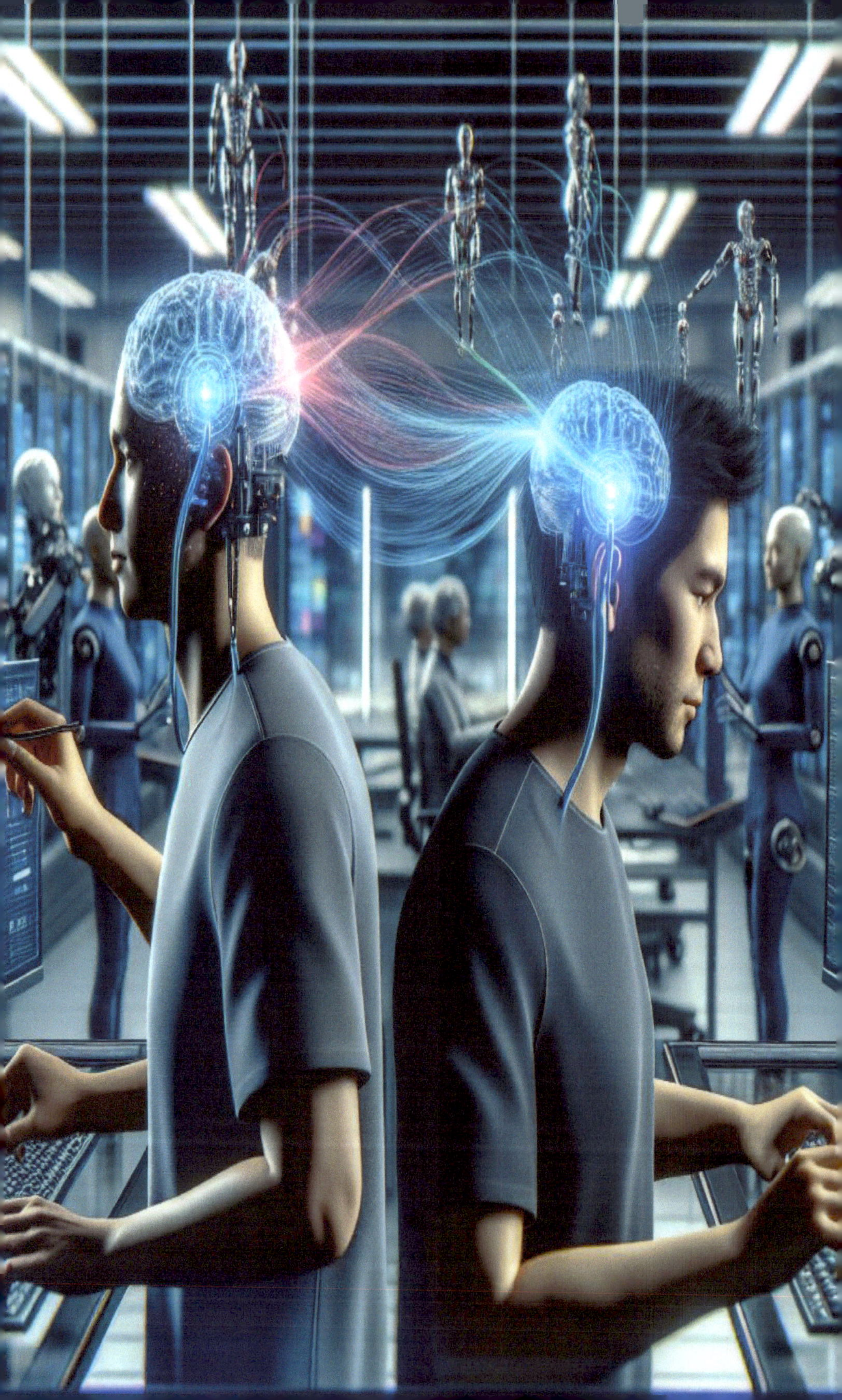

Chapter 5
Neural Alignment

Aligning artificial intelligence (AI) with human cognitive patterns represents one of the most captivating yet daunting challenges in the realm of AI development. Human cognition is a complex interplay of perception, reasoning, memory, and emotions, working together to create a rich tapestry of thought and understanding. In contrast, AI systems operate by processing extensive datasets, recognizing patterns, and making decisions through algorithms. To achieve true alignment between these two domains, we must find innovative ways to connect human thought processes with machine computations.

The idea is not to make AI systems think exactly like humans but rather to develop them in a way that complements and enhances human thought processes. Imagine a system that understands not only what you ask for but the context behind your request, similar to how another person would interpret your words, emotions, and intentions. Such alignment would enable AI to assist humans in ways that feel natural, reducing the learning curve and making collaboration seamless.

One real-world example of this is how virtual assistants like Apple's Siri or Amazon's Alexa are improving their ability to understand not just words but meaning. These systems have evolved from simple command-following machines to tools that try to grasp the intent behind a question. However, this is just the beginning. AI still struggles with tasks that involve abstract thinking, complex decision-making, and understanding the subtleties of human emotions. Aligning AI more closely with human cognition would enable it to perform better in such areas.

In the workplace, AI systems that understand human cognitive patterns could assist in tasks requiring creativity, problem-solving, or collaboration. For example, AI systems might help designers come up with new product ideas by analyzing patterns in consumer behavior and predicting trends. They could assist doctors by quickly processing and analyzing vast amounts of medical data, providing insights that complement the doctor's own expertise.

The trajectory of AI's future will largely depend on how effectively we can harmonize it with the ways humans naturally think and engage with the world. This alignment will be vital in various sectors, including education, healthcare, and interpersonal relationships, where a deeper mutual understanding can lead to richer outcomes. The ultimate vision is to cultivate a partnership where AI not only amplifies human potential but also honors and enriches the uniquely human traits that define our existence. By fostering this synergy, we can ensure that AI serves as a powerful ally, driving us toward a future where innovation and humanity walk hand in hand.

As we explore the alignment between artificial intelligence and human cognitive patterns, several questions arise that guide our understanding and future development in this area: How can we design AI systems that not only replicate human decision-making but also enhance our cognitive abilities? What innovative approaches can we adopt to ensure AI complements rather than mimics human thought processes? As we continue to bridge the gap between AI and human cognition, how can we ensure that AI evolves in a way that respects and nurtures the uniquely human aspects of creativity, empathy, and intuition? These questions provide the foundation for fostering a future where AI and human intelligence coexist, each amplifying the strengths of the other.

Real-Life Example: Revolutionizing Diagnostics

In healthcare, AI tools like PathAI are revolutionizing diagnostics by aligning with human cognitive patterns to enhance the accuracy of medical image analysis. PathAI's deep learning algorithms are trained to recognize patterns in pathology slides, much like how a pathologist would examine them to diagnose diseases such as cancer. These AI systems are designed to learn how human experts interpret and analyze these images, allowing the technology to improve its diagnostic capabilities over time. By closely mirroring human thought processes in recognizing anomalies and patterns in complex medical data, PathAI helps clinicians make faster, more accurate decisions, ultimately improving patient outcomes.

Why It Matters: Aligning AI with human cognitive patterns in fields like healthcare is a game changer. When AI systems can mimic how professionals think, analyze, and diagnose, they can enhance human capabilities and help professionals make more precise decisions faster. In this case, PathAI reduces the cognitive load on pathologists, allowing them to focus on more complex cases and increasing the accuracy of diagnoses. By aligning with the way humans naturally process medical information, AI doesn't just automate the process—it enhances human judgment, ultimately saving time and improving patient care.

Analogy

Think of PathAI as a *mentor* who has studied the methods of the best pathologists. Initially, the mentor observes how experts analyze pathology slides and learns from them. As time progresses, the mentor starts recognizing the subtle patterns and nuances that pathologists use in diagnosing diseases. Over time, this mentor begins to provide diagnostic suggestions that are in line with expert human judgment, making the process faster and more accurate.

Reference: PathAI's AI-powered diagnostic platform and its collaboration with medical professionals (2022)

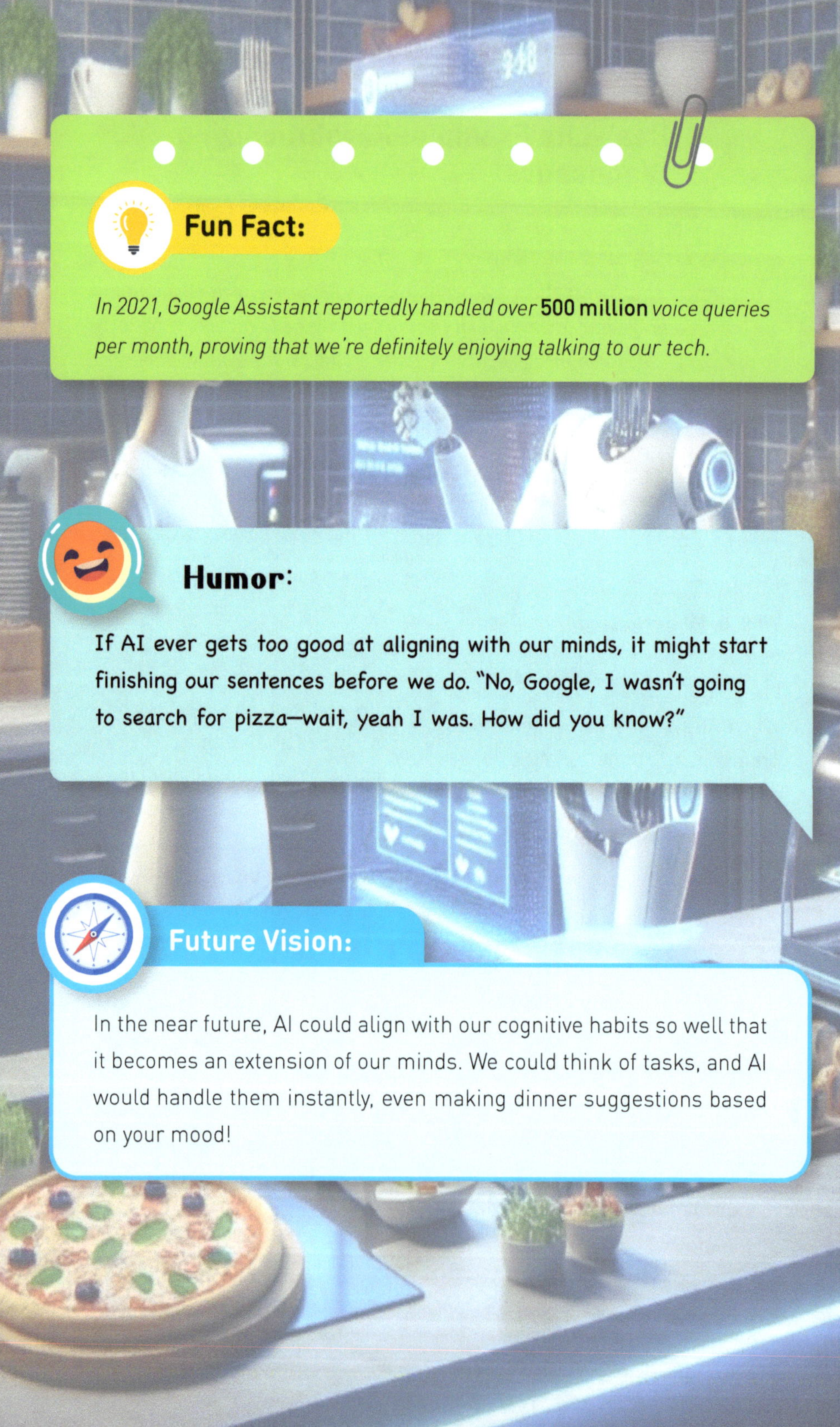

Fun Fact:

In 2021, Google Assistant reportedly handled over **500 million** voice queries per month, proving that we're definitely enjoying talking to our tech.

Humor:

If AI ever gets too good at aligning with our minds, it might start finishing our sentences before we do. "No, Google, I wasn't going to search for pizza—wait, yeah I was. How did you know?"

Future Vision:

In the near future, AI could align with our cognitive habits so well that it becomes an extension of our minds. We could think of tasks, and AI would handle them instantly, even making dinner suggestions based on your mood!

5.2   The brain-machine interface: blurring lines between thought and action

The exploration of brain-machine interfaces (BMIs) stands at the forefront of neuroscience and technology, captivating the imagination by blurring the lines between thought and action. This groundbreaking field is paving the way for a future where controlling machines or communicating with them using merely our thoughts becomes not just a possibility but a reality, driven by advancements in neurotechnology and artificial intelligence.

At its essence, a brain-machine interface facilitates direct communication between the human brain and external devices. This revolutionary approach involves reading neural signals and translating them into actions, allowing individuals to interact with technology in ways previously thought to be the stuff of science fiction. By capturing the electrical impulses generated by neurons, BMIs can interpret our thoughts and convert them into commands that machines can comprehend and execute.

The potential impact of this technology is immense, particularly for those with disabilities. It offers the possibility of restoring mobility and independence to individuals facing significant challenges due to paralysis or other neurodegenerative conditions. By enabling direct control over devices through thought alone, BMIs hold the promise of transforming lives, granting individuals a sense of agency that may have felt lost.

But the implications of brain-machine interfaces extend far beyond medical applications. As this technology continues to evolve, it could revolutionize everyday activities. Imagine a world where we can navigate the digital landscape, communicate, or perform complex tasks without the need for traditional input methods like typing or voice commands. The ability to engage with machines through thought could lead to a more seamless, intuitive interaction, enhancing our daily experiences and productivity.

However, the prospect of blurring the lines between thought and action also invites a host of ethical considerations. The very nature of this technology raises questions about data ownership, privacy, and consent. As our thoughts become accessible to machines, who has the right to access, interpret, or even manipulate that information? Ensuring the security of our mental data is paramount, as is establishing clear guidelines to govern the responsible use of such powerful technologies.

As we venture into this uncharted territory, it is essential to foster a dialogue about the ethical implications surrounding brain-machine interfaces. Balancing innovation with respect for personal privacy will be crucial in shaping a future where these technologies can flourish while preserving the autonomy and dignity of individuals. Navigating these complex questions will be fundamental as we move toward a world where thought and action become intricately intertwined.

As brain-machine interfaces (BMIs) continue to evolve, several intriguing questions arise about their broader implications: What role could BMIs play in enhancing cognitive functions and extending human capabilities beyond their natural limits? How might these technologies change our understanding of consciousness and free will, given their ability to translate thoughts into actions? Could the seamless integration of thought and machine prompt us to redefine what it means to be human, as we merge biological and technological elements? How might BMIs shape industries such as entertainment, education, or even the military, where mental control of machines could redefine the boundaries of human potential? What will be the societal impact as more people adopt such technologies—could it lead to a digital divide or increase inequality between those with access to advanced BMIs and those without? These questions challenge us to think deeply about the intersection of neuroscience, ethics, and technology, guiding the development of BMIs in a way that maximizes their potential while considering the human experience.

Real-Life Example: Neuralink

Neuralink is pushing the boundaries of technology by working on a brain-computer interface that connects your brain directly to devices. Imagine being able to control your smartphone, computer, or even prosthetic limbs, just by thinking about it. It's like turning your thoughts into keyboard shortcuts, where you don't need to lift a finger—your mind becomes the controller. This cutting-edge technology has the potential to revolutionize how we interact with the digital world, offering unprecedented levels of control and accessibility, especially for individuals with disabilities.

Why It Matters: Neuralink represents a huge leap forward in how we interact with technology, aligning our brain's natural processes with digital systems. This connection could not only make our interactions with devices faster and more intuitive but also provide life-changing opportunities for people with motor impairments or neurological conditions. The potential applications—from controlling prosthetics to perhaps even enhancing human cognition—could profoundly reshape medicine, accessibility, and human-computer interaction as we know it.

Reference: Neuralink's official website and ongoing research updates.

Analogy

Think of Neuralink as a *translator* between your brain and the digital world. Just as a translator helps you communicate with someone who speaks a different language, Neuralink translates the electrical signals in your brain into commands that devices can understand. Over time, it's like having a personal assistant that responds to your thoughts, seamlessly carrying out tasks without the need for physical input.

Fun Fact:

Elon Musk's Neuralink has already demonstrated this tech with a monkey playing Pong using only its brain! It's both amazing and a little bit sci-fi.

Humor:

So, in the future, you could change the TV channel with just a thought. But what happens when you're thinking of two different shows? AI better be a good mind-reader.

Future Vision:

We're heading toward a future where people could control entire computer systems and robots through thoughts alone. Imagine people with disabilities operating smart homes or individuals working at superhuman speeds by directly interfacing with machines.

5.3   Advances in neurotechnology and AI synchronization

Recent developments in neurotechnology and artificial intelligence (AI) are reshaping how we interact with machines, leading to exciting new possibilities that can enhance our daily lives. Neurotechnology encompasses various tools and methods that connect with the brain to observe and influence its activities. When we combine this with AI, we unlock the potential to transform many areas, including healthcare, communication, and even entertainment.

One of the most significant advancements in this field is how AI can read and interpret brain signals more accurately. Our brains generate an enormous amount of data, which can be overwhelming for traditional analysis methods. However, AI algorithms are designed to sift through this information quickly and efficiently, uncovering patterns that were previously difficult to detect. This ability is crucial for developing brain-machine interfaces and other neurotechnological applications. For example, researchers can use AI to decode a person's thoughts or emotions based on their neural activity, leading to a deeper understanding of how the brain functions and how it interacts with the world around us.

In addition to understanding brain activity, AI is making waves in the field of neuroprosthetics, which are artificial limbs or devices controlled directly by signals from the brain. Thanks to advancements in AI technology, these devices are becoming increasingly sophisticated. For instance, modern neuroprosthetics can now provide users with feedback, such as the sensation of touch or pressure. This connection creates a more natural and intuitive experience for users, allowing them to interact with their prosthetic limbs as if they were their own. This progress marks a significant step toward achieving true synchronization between human biology and artificial systems, highlighting how technology can enhance human capabilities.

Moreover, the synchronization between neurotechnology and AI opens doors to new therapeutic possibilities. For example, AI can analyze brain patterns to create personalized treatment plans for individuals with neurological disorders. By examining how a person's brain behaves over time, AI can help predict when they might experience symptoms of conditions like epilepsy or depression. This proactive approach allows for timely interventions, enabling healthcare providers to respond before symptoms escalate. By focusing on prevention rather than merely treating issues as they arise, we can revolutionize mental health care and improve patients' quality of life.

As we look to the future, researchers are exploring ways to deepen the connection between AI and our brains even further. They are investigating how AI can enhance cognitive functions such as memory and learning. Imagine a world where we can boost our ability to remember information or acquire new skills rapidly. This exploration raises the fascinating idea that one day, we might be able to "upload" information directly into our brains. This concept, once confined to science fiction, could fundamentally change how we learn and retain knowledge. Picture a future where students can learn complex subjects in a fraction of the time it currently takes, simply by accessing information directly through a brain-machine interface.

The implications of these advancements extend beyond individual benefits. As neurotechnology and AI continue to evolve, they have the potential to impact society at large. For instance, imagine a workplace where employees can enhance their productivity and creativity through direct brain-to-machine communication. In this environment, workers could collaborate seamlessly with AI systems to solve complex problems, generate innovative ideas, and execute tasks more efficiently. This could lead to an era of unprecedented human productivity, where we work hand-in-hand with intelligent machines to push the boundaries of what we can achieve.

However, with these advancements come important ethical considerations. As we begin to blur the lines between human cognition and machine intelligence, we must carefully navigate issues related to privacy, consent, and security. Who owns the data generated by brain-machine interactions? How can we ensure that this information is protected from misuse? These questions will require thoughtful discussions and regulations as we move forward in this exciting field.

As the fusion of neurotechnology and AI unfolds, we are presented with a new set of possibilities that challenge our perceptions of human potential. How far can we push the boundaries of human cognition with the help of AI—could we one day synchronize our minds with machines so seamlessly that learning and creativity become instantaneous? As AI becomes more adept at interacting with our brainwaves, how might we safeguard the delicate balance between empowering individuals and maintaining ethical integrity? These questions push us to imagine a future where the line between what is human and what is artificial becomes increasingly blurred, yet grounded in principles that preserve our autonomy and humanity.

In conclusion, the potential for neurotechnology and AI synchronization is immense. As we continue to explore and develop these technologies, we are likely to witness profound changes in how we interact with machines, enhance our cognitive abilities, and ultimately, redefine what it means to be human in a technology-driven world. The journey ahead is filled with possibilities, and as we embrace these advancements, we must also remain vigilant about the ethical implications they entail, ensuring a future that benefits all of humanity.

Real-Life Example: BrainGate

BrainGate is a groundbreaking neurotechnology that enables individuals with paralysis to control devices and computers directly with their minds. By using a brain-computer interface, the system interprets brain signals and translates them into commands for external devices like prosthetics or a computer cursor. It's as if the brain's natural signals are converted into digital actions, providing those with limited mobility the ability to interact with the world in ways that were once unimaginable. This technology is not just about innovation—it's about creating new opportunities for communication, mobility, and independence.

Why It Matters: BrainGate is a monumental leap in both medicine and technology, as it creates the possibility for people with severe disabilities to regain lost independence. By blending AI with human thought, it bypasses physical limitations and opens up a new realm of possibilities for mobility and communication. This system doesn't just help users interact with technology; it gives them back a sense of control and autonomy in their everyday lives, empowering them to do things many thought were out of reach.

Reference: BrainGate's pioneering work in brain-computer interfaces and neurotechnology.

Analogy

Think of BrainGate as a *bridge* between your thoughts and the digital world. Imagine trying to control a remote-controlled car using only your thoughts—the car moves, but instead of using a joystick, your mind sends signals to direct its movements. BrainGate works in a similar way, turning the electrical impulses in your brain into actionable commands for computers or prosthetics, allowing you to control the technology directly.

Fun Fact:

*One BrainGate user typed out sentences at **90 characters per minute**, just by thinking! That's faster than some of us type with both hands.*

Humor:

Neurotechnology may soon help you think your way through emails. One day, instead of saying, "Sorry for the delayed response," you could be typing it out with your mind—no excuses!

Future Vision:

AI and neurotechnology could soon synchronize in ways that allow people to use their brains for everything from complex medical surgeries to flying drones just by thinking about it.

5.4　Creating seamless collaboration: achieving neural synergy

The vision of combining neurotechnology and artificial intelligence (AI) aims to achieve what is known as neural synergy. This concept revolves around creating a seamless collaboration between human cognitive functions and machine intelligence, allowing for a smooth and intuitive exchange of information. In simpler terms, neural synergy means finding a way for humans and machines to work together in a manner that feels completely natural.

Imagine a world where you no longer need to rely on physical interfaces like keyboards or mice. Instead, you could simply think about a task, and the AI would instantly understand your intent and execute it. This revolutionary form of collaboration has the potential to transform numerous fields, particularly those where creativity and rapid iteration are essential. For instance, designers could use neural synergy to brainstorm ideas with AI, allowing them to explore multiple design possibilities effortlessly and refine their concepts in real time.

In the realm of creative arts, the exploration of neural synergy is already underway. Innovative AI systems are being designed to collaborate with musicians, visual artists, and writers. Rather than replacing human creators, these systems act as partners, enriching the creative process. By offering suggestions, generating content, or providing insights based on the creator's input, AI can enhance the creative journey, opening up new avenues for artistic expression. This collaboration can result in unique works of art that blend human intuition with machine precision, pushing the boundaries of creativity.

However, the journey toward achieving true neural synergy is not without its hurdles. One of the foremost challenges lies in ensuring that AI systems can grasp the subtleties and complexities of human thought. Human cognition is intricate, influenced by emotions, context, and cultural backgrounds. To achieve meaningful collaboration, AI must learn to interpret these nuances effectively.

Additionally, maintaining control over AI systems while granting them enough autonomy for productive collaboration is crucial. Striking the right balance between guidance and independence is essential for fostering a productive partnership.

Despite these obstacles, the potential advantages of achieving neural synergy are vast. In the educational sector, for instance, AI-powered tutors could revolutionize how students learn. By adapting to individual learning styles and preferences with remarkable precision, AI can provide tailored support, ensuring that each learner receives the guidance they need to thrive. This personalized approach could enhance educational outcomes and help students reach their full potential.

In healthcare, the integration of neural synergy could lead to significant advancements. Imagine surgeons equipped with AI systems that can analyze real-time data during complex operations, providing insights and recommendations as they navigate intricate procedures. This collaboration could not only improve surgical outcomes but also empower medical professionals to make informed decisions more efficiently, ultimately saving lives and enhancing patient care.

As we strive for this seamless collaboration between humans and machines, we must also consider the ethical implications of such technology. Establishing trust and transparency in AI systems is paramount. We need to ensure that users feel comfortable relying on AI to support their creative and professional endeavors while safeguarding their autonomy and privacy.

In conclusion, the pursuit of neural synergy represents an exciting frontier in the relationship between humans and machines. By fostering seamless collaboration, we have the potential to unlock innovative solutions, enhance creativity, and improve various aspects of life. As we navigate this journey, it is essential to address the technical and ethical challenges that lie ahead, ensuring that we create a future where humans and AI can thrive together harmoniously.

Real-Life Example: AI-Assisted Surgery

The **da Vinci Surgical System** is revolutionizing the field of surgery by combining robotics with AI to offer unparalleled precision and control. This robotic platform allows surgeons to perform complex procedures with enhanced dexterity and minimal invasiveness, all while being guided by AI-driven insights. Imagine a surgeon using robotic arms that can move with the precision of a fine-tuned instrument, yet with a level of control and steadiness that is often beyond human capabilities. It's as though the surgeon's hands are augmented with superhuman abilities, making intricate surgeries safer and more effective than ever before.

Why It Matters: AI-assisted surgery is a game-changer, as it significantly enhances a surgeon's ability to perform complex procedures with greater accuracy and fewer risks. This technology provides a new level of control, reducing human error and leading to faster recovery times for patients. By aligning AI's precision with human expertise, it paves the way for safer surgeries, more successful outcomes, and a future where minimally invasive procedures can tackle even the most challenging medical conditions.

Reference: da Vinci Surgical System and AI-assisted surgery advancements in medical robotics.

Analogy

Think of the da Vinci Surgical System as a *superpowered extension* of the surgeon's hands. It's like upgrading a human craftsman's tools with cutting-edge technology that not only makes their movements more precise but also provides real-time feedback and assistance. The AI acts as a trusted partner, ensuring that every incision, stitch, and maneuver is carried out with the utmost accuracy, improving outcomes in delicate surgeries.

Fun Fact:

*Robotic-assisted surgeries using AI have a **96% success rate** for procedures like prostatectomies, far surpassing traditional methods.*

Humor:

In the future, surgeons might have to explain to their patients, "Don't worry, it wasn't me—it was my robot sidekick!"

Future Vision:

Neural synergy between humans and AI could open up new ways of working, where brain-machine interfaces allow for split-second collaboration on tasks that previously required extensive manual control.

5.5   Overcoming the challenges of bias and control in AI alignment

As we strive to align artificial intelligence (AI) with human thinking and achieve what's known as neural synergy, we face significant challenges, especially when it comes to bias and control within AI systems. The effectiveness of AI largely depends on the data it learns from. If that data contains biases—whether intentional or not—the AI will likely mirror those biases in its decisions and actions. This can lead to outcomes that are not just unfair, but harmful to individuals and communities.

Bias in AI can appear in various ways. For instance, facial recognition technology might struggle to accurately identify people from certain ethnic backgrounds, resulting in misidentifications and potentially dangerous situations. Similarly, hiring algorithms that are meant to streamline the recruitment process can inadvertently favor candidates based on gender or race, reinforcing existing disparities in the workplace. Addressing these biases is not just a technical challenge; it is a moral obligation. To successfully integrate AI into our daily lives, we must ensure that these systems operate fairly and justly.

Control is another important aspect when discussing AI alignment. As AI systems gain more autonomy, it raises critical questions about oversight and accountability. Who should be in control of these intelligent systems, and how much independence should they have? As these systems learn from their experiences and adapt, we must ensure that their behaviors align with our human values and ethical standards. This concern becomes even more pressing in high-stakes scenarios where AI decisions can significantly impact people's lives, such as in healthcare, law enforcement, and finance.

To tackle these challenges, one effective strategy is to implement robust ethical frameworks in the development of AI technologies. Such frameworks should prioritize transparency and accountability, clarifying how decisions are made and who is responsible for those choices. It's essential that we cultivate a culture of responsibility among AI developers and researchers, ensuring that ethical considerations remain at the forefront of their work.

Additionally, diversifying the datasets used to train AI systems is crucial. By including a wider range of perspectives and experiences in the training data, we can reduce bias and create more representative systems. This means actively seeking out voices that have historically been marginalized or overlooked in technology development, ensuring that the AI we build reflects the diversity of the world we inhabit. When we include different viewpoints, we enrich the AI's ability to understand and serve a broader audience.

Ultimately, the success of aligning AI with human cognitive patterns depends on our ability to address these challenges head-on. We need to create systems that not only perform tasks efficiently but also do so in a manner that is ethical, fair, and aligned with the diverse values of humanity. By focusing on reducing bias and ensuring effective control, we can pave the way for a future where AI complements human capabilities, enhancing our decision-making while respecting our varied perspectives and ethical standards.

As we move forward, it is essential for all stakeholders—developers, policymakers, and the general public—to engage in ongoing discussions about these critical issues. By fostering a collaborative dialogue, we can work together to ensure that AI technology serves humanity in a positive way, promoting a society where innovation and ethical considerations coexist harmoniously.

In conclusion, overcoming the challenges of bias and control in AI alignment is not merely a technical hurdle but a vital societal goal. As we navigate this complex landscape, we must remain vigilant and committed to creating AI systems that truly reflect our shared values and aspirations. Together, we can build a future where AI empowers us and enhances our lives, all while being fair and just.

Real-Life Example: Bias in Facial Recognition

Facial recognition technology, while groundbreaking, has faced significant challenges with bias, especially in the misidentification of individuals from minority groups. In some cases, these systems have been less accurate at recognizing people with darker skin tones or those from diverse ethnic backgrounds. This has sparked debates around the fairness and ethical implications of using such technology in law enforcement and other sectors. To address these issues, there's a growing push to realign AI systems with ethical standards, ensuring that facial recognition algorithms are trained to be more inclusive and fair for all individuals, regardless of race or ethnicity.

Analogy

Imagine a *portrait artist* who paints hundreds of faces but only focuses on a narrow range of subjects—let's say only light-skinned individuals. When asked to create portraits of people from different backgrounds, the artist struggles to capture the nuances, leading to misrepresentations. In the same way, facial recognition AI systems, if not trained with diverse data, can have trouble identifying individuals from underrepresented groups accurately. The solution? Broaden the training data to better reflect the diversity of the population, just as the artist would learn to portray a wider range of faces more accurately.

Why It Matters: The biases in facial recognition technology can have serious consequences, especially in critical applications like security, hiring, and law enforcement. Misidentification can lead to unfair treatment or even wrongful accusations. By aligning AI more closely with ethical standards, we can create systems that are fairer, more accurate, and better able to serve all individuals equally. Ensuring fairness in algorithms not only improves the accuracy of the technology but also builds trust with users, paving the way for AI to be used responsibly in society.

Reference: Alan Turing's foundational work on ethics and AI. Turing.org.uk

Fun Fact:

In 2019, research found that facial recognition systems misidentified people of color at rates up to **10 times higher** *than for white individuals. Companies are working hard to solve these issues.*

Humor:

Facial recognition might become too friendly one day. Imagine walking into a store and the AI goes, "Hello again! How about buying that shirt you were eyeing last time?"

Future Vision:

AI systems could be developed to constantly audit themselves, checking for biases and refining their algorithms to align with human values—much like having a digital conscience that guides its actions.

Scaling human collaration
Scaling human capabilities fough Amutication
AI- um
Learning

Chapter **6**

Symbiotic Peak

The concept of collaboration between humans and artificial intelligence (AI) is not just a futuristic idea; it's a transformative reality that promises to reshape our world. This partnership envisions a future where both humans and AI work together seamlessly, leveraging their unique strengths to achieve remarkable outcomes that neither could accomplish alone.

At the core of this collaboration lies the recognition of what each party brings to the table. Humans possess creativity, emotional intelligence, and complex decision-making capabilities, which are crucial in navigating the intricacies of life. We can think abstractly, empathize with others, and adapt to new and unexpected situations. On the other hand, AI excels in processing vast amounts of data at lightning speed, automating repetitive tasks, and optimizing overall performance through analytics and insights.

The true power of this partnership becomes evident when these strengths are combined. Consider a scenario where a surgeon is performing a complex operation alongside an AI system. In this setting, the AI does not replace the surgeon; rather, it acts as a sophisticated assistant, providing real-time insights and recommendations drawn from an extensive database of similar surgeries. While the surgeon relies on their training and experience to navigate the emotional and intricate aspects of the procedure, the AI ensures that every detail is accounted for, helping the surgeon explore all possible options.

This collaborative approach not only enhances the surgeon's capabilities but also minimizes the risk of errors, ultimately leading to better outcomes for patients.

In today's workplaces, the integration of human-AI collaboration is becoming increasingly common. From advanced digital marketing tools that analyze consumer behavior to autonomous vehicles that operate alongside drivers, AI is now a crucial part of daily tasks. This integration allows professionals to focus on high-level strategic decisions rather than getting bogged down by routine responsibilities. Take the finance sector as an example: financial analysts can now use AI-powered tools to sift through extensive datasets, identifying trends and patterns quickly and efficiently. This capability frees them to concentrate on strategic forecasting and informed decision-making, adding value to their roles.

In this envisioned future, humans are not competing against AI; instead, they are enhancing their own capabilities through its support. The partnership creates a new paradigm where both parties coexist and thrive, leading to breakthroughs that could redefine industries and improve lives.

Moreover, this collaboration extends into research and development, where AI assists scientists in accelerating discovery processes, analyzing complex datasets, and even generating hypotheses. In creative fields, artists are beginning to work alongside AI tools that can suggest new concepts or help refine their work, ultimately enriching the creative process.

As we move forward, nurturing this partnership will be essential. It involves not just understanding how to utilize AI effectively but also fostering an environment where both humans and machines can learn from one another. By embracing this symbiotic relationship, we can unlock new levels of potential, creativity, and innovation, paving the way for a future that is more interconnected and collaborative than ever before.

In conclusion, maximizing human-AI collaboration is not merely about enhancing productivity; it is about redefining what we can achieve together. This partnership can drive us towards a future filled with opportunities, creativity, and shared success, allowing humanity to flourish in ways we have yet to fully realize.

Real-Life Example: Personalized Medicine

In the field of *personalized medicine*, AI is revolutionizing how we approach patient care, particularly for those with rare genetic diseases. The AI platform *Tempus* uses machine learning to analyze vast amounts of genetic data, clinical records, and treatment outcomes. By learning from thousands of patient profiles, the system helps doctors predict the most effective treatments tailored to an individual's specific genetic makeup. For instance, Tempus recently partnered with oncologists to analyze cancer patients' genetic data and create personalized cancer treatment plans that target the tumor's genetic mutations. The AI system constantly learns from new patient data, improving its predictions and assisting doctors in making more informed decisions. The result is a collaborative process where AI acts as an invaluable advisor, continuously refining its suggestions, while human expertise guides the final treatment plan.

Why It Matters: This collaboration is especially important because it addresses the growing need for personalized healthcare. Traditional one-size-fits-all approaches to medicine often fall short, especially when treating complex or rare diseases. By combining AI's ability to analyze massive datasets with a doctor's nuanced understanding of the patient's needs, we move toward more precise, effective, and individualized treatment plans. This not only improves the quality of care for patients but also opens up new possibilities for treating conditions that were once difficult to understand or treat.

Reference: AI in personalized medicine.
https://www.tempus.com/

Analogy

Imagine a *master chef* crafting a dish from a unique set of ingredients. The chef is experienced, knowing how flavors combine and how to perfect each dish. But imagine the chef is also assisted by an AI-powered ingredient database that suggests new flavor combinations and cooking techniques based on the chef's specific needs and previous successes. The AI doesn't cook the dish itself but offers insights and recommendations that complement the chef's expertise, enabling them to create a far more intricate and personalized meal than they could alone. Similarly, in *personalized medicine*, the doctor (the master chef) relies on AI to suggest tailored treatments, but ultimately the human expert refines the plan based on experience and understanding of the patient.

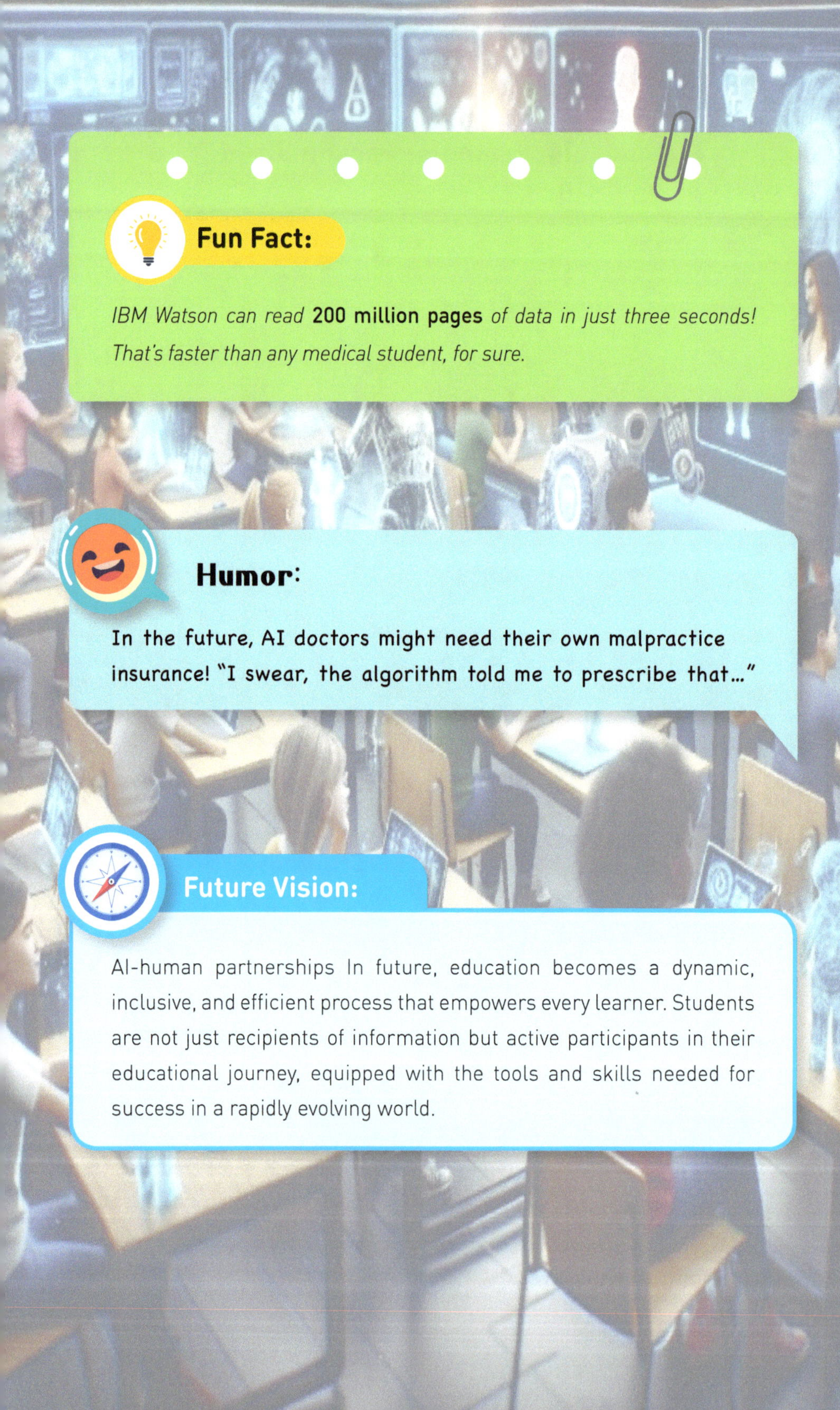

Fun Fact:

IBM Watson can read **200 million pages** of data in just three seconds! That's faster than any medical student, for sure.

Humor:

In the future, AI doctors might need their own malpractice insurance! "I swear, the algorithm told me to prescribe that…"

Future Vision:

AI-human partnerships In future, education becomes a dynamic, inclusive, and efficient process that empowers every learner. Students are not just recipients of information but active participants in their educational journey, equipped with the tools and skills needed for success in a rapidly evolving world.

6.2 How Symbiotic Systems Redefine Work, Learning, and Innovation

As symbiotic AI systems continue to evolve, they are dramatically reshaping how we approach work, learning, and innovation. Historically, both professional environments and educational frameworks have adhered to strict, traditional structures—fixed job roles, uniform educational pathways, and clearly delineated tasks. However, the advent of symbiotic AI challenges these conventions, paving the way for dynamic, personalized, and adaptive environments that can change in real-time.

In the workplace, AI is fundamentally transforming job functions across a multitude of industries. For instance, in manufacturing, AI-powered robots collaborate alongside human workers on the production floor. Rather than replacing people, these machines serve as valuable assistants in tasks requiring precision or heavy lifting. This collaboration allows human workers to redirect their efforts toward more creative and complex responsibilities, such as design and problem-solving. As a result, the workforce becomes more efficient and adaptable, capable of tackling challenges that were previously beyond reach.

In the realm of education, AI-driven platforms are revolutionizing the learning experience. Traditional classrooms often adopt a one-size-fits-all approach, but symbiotic AI systems offer tailored learning experiences that cater to each student's individual needs. By analyzing a student's learning patterns, AI can craft customized learning paths that help address weaknesses while enhancing their strengths. This personalized approach not only boosts academic performance but also fosters a deeper engagement with the material.

When it comes to innovation, symbiotic AI systems unlock an entirely new realm of possibilities. In research and development, AI accelerates the discovery process by sifting through vast datasets and identifying patterns that might elude human researchers. For example, in drug discovery, AI has proven instrumental in identifying new compounds and predicting their effectiveness, significantly speeding up the timeline for bringing innovative treatments to market.

In conclusion, the rise of symbiotic AI systems is not just transforming the way we work, learn, and innovate—it's rewriting the very blueprint of how we interact with the world around us. As AI and humans increasingly collaborate, we are stepping into a future where rigid job roles, one-size-fits-all education, and static innovation processes are no longer the norm. Instead, we are embracing fluid, adaptive systems that evolve in real-time, offering a new level of personalization and creativity. In the workplace, AI isn't here to replace us, but to empower us—freeing up human potential to tackle the complex, the creative, and the unprecedented. In education, it's not about fitting students into a predefined mold, but unlocking a learning journey as unique as each individual. And in innovation, AI is accelerating breakthroughs that were once the stuff of dreams. But as we venture into this exciting new era, important questions loom: How do we strike the right balance between AI assistance and human ingenuity? Can we ensure that these powerful systems serve humanity's best interests, not just its efficiency? And as we chart this new frontier, how can we cultivate a future where both human and machine intelligence are not just collaborators, but co-creators of something extraordinary? The possibilities are endless, but the path forward requires us to think, adapt, and innovate— together.

Real-Life Example: AI Tutoring Systems

AI-powered tutoring systems, such as *Duolingo*, are transforming language learning by providing personalized, real-time feedback to students. Duolingo's AI system adapts to each learner's pace, identifying their strengths and weaknesses to offer tailored lessons. As learners progress, the AI adjusts the difficulty of tasks, helping users gradually build proficiency. What's remarkable is that Duolingo can offer a dynamic and interactive learning experience, constantly refining its approach based on each individual's responses. It's like having an ever-patient tutor who not only guides you through lessons but also adapts to your learning style, ensuring the journey is both engaging and effective.

Why It Matters: AI tutoring systems have the potential to revolutionize education by making personalized learning accessible to everyone, everywhere. Unlike traditional classrooms, where the pace is often set for the average learner, AI can tailor lessons to each individual's needs. This adaptability ensures that learners don't fall behind or get stuck in one-size-fits-all methods. For language learning, in particular, this means quicker retention, a deeper understanding of grammar and vocabulary, and, ultimately, more fluent speakers. As AI evolves, the ability to provide individualized instruction will expand across other subjects, democratizing education and offering students the best path forward in their learning journey.

Reference: AI-driven language learning insights. https://www.duolingo.com/

Analogy

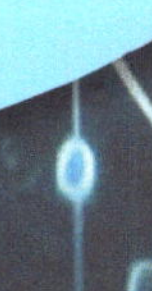

Think of it as *a dance instructor* who watches your every move and adjusts the tempo and difficulty of the routine based on your skill level. If you're struggling to keep up with a step, the instructor slows it down and offers tips, and if you're mastering the moves quickly, they add complexity to the routine to keep you challenged. Just like that, Duolingo and other AI tutoring systems adjust the pace of learning and provide feedback, ensuring you're always engaged, but not overwhelmed—creating a rhythm of learning that's perfect for you.

 **Fun Fact:**

*Research shows that students using AI tutoring systems are learning at rates **30% faster** than those with traditional methods. Goodbye, boring textbooks!*

 **Humor:**

AI might get so good at tutoring that future students will beg, "Can't I just have one day off? You never get tired!"

 **Future Vision:**

In the future, AI could redefine entire education systems. Instead of traditional classrooms, we might have AI-tailored curriculums for each student, allowing them to learn at their own pace with constant, personalized feedback.

6.3   Scaling Human Capabilities Through AI Augmentation

AI augmentation is fundamentally about enhancing human capabilities by integrating artificial intelligence into various aspects of our lives. This approach transforms what were once seen as limitations into newfound strengths, empowering individuals to accomplish tasks that might have previously seemed time-consuming, challenging, or even impossible. Importantly, this doesn't imply that humans are becoming obsolete; instead, AI serves as a powerful extension of human capabilities, allowing us to reach new heights.

In the healthcare sector, for example, AI is revolutionizing how doctors analyze medical images. These AI systems can process thousands of images in mere seconds, spotting patterns and anomalies that might escape the keenest human eye. This rapid analysis not only speeds up the diagnostic process but also enhances accuracy, enabling healthcare professionals to dedicate more time to direct patient care rather than being bogged down by administrative tasks.

Similarly, in the logistics industry, companies like Amazon leverage AI to streamline their operations. By optimizing delivery routes, predicting customer demand, and effectively managing inventory, AI enables these businesses to operate more efficiently than ever before. This not only saves time and resources but also improves overall service quality, benefiting customers in the process.

The impact of AI augmentation is also felt in creative fields, where artists and musicians are beginning to harness the power of AI in intriguing ways. For instance, musicians are using AI to compose new music, while visual artists experiment with AI-generated artwork. Rather than replacing human creativity, these tools provide fresh avenues for exploration and innovation. An artist might input their ideas into an AI program, which then generates multiple versions of a piece, sparking new directions and inspiration that the artist may not have considered otherwise.

In terms of personal productivity, AI tools like virtual assistants and automation systems are helping individuals manage their time and tasks more effectively. These systems can schedule meetings, send reminders, and even analyze how a person allocates their time, offering insightful suggestions for improvement. By taking over mundane and repetitive tasks, AI enables people to concentrate on what truly matters, whether that's pursuing work projects, engaging in hobbies, or spending quality time with loved ones.

Ultimately, scaling human capabilities through AI is not about fostering dependency on machines; it's about creating a symbiotic relationship where each complements the other's strengths. With the help of AI augmentation, individuals can tackle challenges that once felt insurmountable, unlocking new opportunities for personal growth and achievement. As we embrace this partnership with AI, we step into a future brimming with possibilities, where human potential is amplified and enriched by the innovative power of technology.

In conclusion, AI augmentation is not just about enhancing what we do—it's about unlocking what we *can* do. It's about taking the limits of human potential and expanding them, turning the impossible into the achievable. AI is not here to replace us—it's here to partner with us, to free us from mundane tasks and give us the space to focus on what truly matters: innovation, creativity, and human connection. The future is unfolding before us, and with AI augmenting our abilities, we are poised to achieve more than ever before. But the question is—how will we use this power? What kind of future will we build together, where human and machine work hand in hand to create something truly extraordinary? The possibilities are limitless, but the choice is ours.

Real-Life Example: Exoskeletons

AI-powered exoskeletons are transforming industries like manufacturing and logistics by enhancing human strength and endurance. These wearable robotic suits are designed to assist workers by providing extra support and enabling them to lift heavy loads with ease. For example, *Ekso Bionics* has developed an exoskeleton that helps workers in warehouses and factories reduce physical strain while performing repetitive or physically demanding tasks. The AI in these exoskeletons learns from the user's movements and adapts in real-time to optimize their strength and posture, making even the heaviest lifting feel effortless. It's as if workers have been given a set of superhuman muscles, all thanks to a powerful, adaptive AI system that works alongside them.

Why It Matters: AI-powered exoskeletons are not just about making physically demanding work easier; they're also about improving worker safety and reducing injury. By providing real-time support, these suits prevent strain and fatigue, which are common causes of long-term injuries in physically intense jobs. This innovation is revolutionizing industries by making it possible for workers to perform at their best without compromising their health. With AI continuously improving the suit's responsiveness, we're seeing a future where human strength is no longer limited by biology, and physically demanding tasks become safer and more efficient.

Analogy

Imagine a *superhero suit* that enhances your physical abilities the moment you put it on. Just like how Iron Man's suit boosts his strength and power, an AI-powered exoskeleton serves as a real-world version of that—amplifying human capabilities to handle intense physical work. The AI within the exoskeleton adjusts and refines its support, ensuring that each movement is more efficient and less strenuous. It's like having a personal trainer who tailors their coaching to you, allowing you to push past physical limits without breaking a sweat.

Reference: AI exoskeletons for industrial use.
https://www.eskobionics.com/

Fun Fact:

The U.S. military is actively developing AI-powered exoskeletons for soldiers, which may soon allow them to run faster and carry heavier loads in the field.

Humor:

In the future, people might wear AI-powered exosuits just to get through Black Friday shopping—no more getting trampled for the last deal!

Future Vision:

AI could enhance human capabilities beyond just physical strength. Imagine mental augmentation, where AI helps humans process complex information at lightning speed, making tasks like coding or research feel like child's play.

6.4   Case Studies of Successful Human–AI Symbiosis in Industry

Across various industries, remarkable examples of successful human-AI symbiosis highlight the incredible potential of collaboration between humans and intelligent machines. This partnership is not only transforming operations but also enhancing the way we work, make decisions, and serve customers.

One standout case is found in the automotive industry, particularly with companies like Tesla. They have taken the lead in integrating AI into the development of semi-autonomous vehicles. For instance, in Tesla's Model S, AI plays a crucial role in assisting with tasks such as changing lanes, parking, and even navigating on highways. The AI system continuously analyzes real-time data from its sensors, enabling it to understand the driving environment, detect obstacles, and predict the behavior of other road users. While the AI functions as a helpful co-pilot, the human driver retains full control, enhancing both safety and convenience. This partnership allows drivers to enjoy a more relaxed driving experience while benefiting from AI's real-time analysis and decision-making capabilities. Additionally, as Tesla vehicles gather data from millions of miles driven, the AI continually learns and improves, becoming more adept over time at anticipating and responding to complex driving situations.

In the retail sector, brands like Zara and H&M are harnessing AI to gain a competitive edge by predicting trends and optimizing their supply chains. These companies employ AI systems that analyze a variety of data, including customer preferences, social media trends, and sales figures. By understanding these insights, brands can make informed decisions about which products to produce and in what quantities. For example, Zara can quickly adapt to changing fashion trends, ensuring that its inventory reflects current consumer demand. This proactive approach not only minimizes waste but also ensures that customers find the right products at the right time. In this dynamic environment, human designers and managers collaborate closely with AI systems, using the valuable data provided to refine their strategies and improve offerings. As a result, both creativity and efficiency thrive, enabling these companies to remain agile in a competitive market.

The financial sector is another area where human-AI collaboration shines. In this field, AI is increasingly utilized to analyze markets, forecast trends, and manage investments. Hedge funds like Renaissance Technologies employ sophisticated AI algorithms to execute high-frequency trades, uncovering patterns in the market that may go unnoticed by human traders. These AI systems can rapidly process vast amounts of data in real-time, enabling them to make split-second decisions that can lead to significant profits. However, human traders and analysts remain vital to the process. They oversee the AI's activities and make necessary adjustments to investment strategies based on market conditions, ensuring that the AI operates within ethical and regulatory frameworks. This collaborative approach not only enhances the accuracy of trading decisions but also helps mitigate risks, leading to better overall performance in investment portfolios.

Another interesting example can be found in healthcare, where human-AI collaboration is making strides in diagnostics and patient care. AI algorithms analyze medical data, such as patient histories, lab results, and imaging studies, to assist doctors in making faster and more accurate diagnoses. For instance, AI-powered imaging tools can detect early signs of conditions like cancer, often with greater precision than human radiologists. This enables healthcare professionals to identify and address health issues more promptly, ultimately improving patient outcomes. Moreover, AI can help personalize treatment plans by analyzing individual patient data and suggesting tailored therapies, allowing doctors to provide more effective care.

The potential is vast, but with it comes the responsibility to ensure that as we deepen our collaboration with machines, we don't lose sight of our ethical obligations and human values. As we continue to explore these possibilities, we must ask ourselves: How can we ensure this partnership between humans and AI is a force for good, enhancing innovation, creativity, and human well-being? The future of human-AI collaboration is bright, but only if we approach it with intention and foresight.

Real-Life Example: Farming with Drones

Farmers are embracing AI-powered drones to revolutionize agriculture by monitoring crop health, optimizing irrigation, and even predicting yields. Companies like *DJI* and *Raven Industries* have developed advanced drone systems that gather real-time data from the air, allowing farmers to assess their crops' condition from a bird's-eye view. These drones use AI to analyze the collected data, detecting issues like water stress, pest infestations, or nutrient deficiencies, and can even automate irrigation to ensure crops get just the right amount of water. It's like equipping farmers with an aerial assistant who never tires and can survey vast fields in minutes, all from the comfort of their tractor or mobile device.

Analogy

Imagine being given *a fleet of flying scouts* that keep watch over your entire farm. Instead of walking the fields, checking each plant by hand, these drones work tirelessly overhead, sending detailed reports on crop conditions directly to you. Think of it like having a drone-powered *satellite system* in your backyard, offering real-time insights about your crops' health and the best strategies to boost productivity. The drones continuously adapt to changing conditions, ensuring farmers can make timely decisions that lead to higher yields and more efficient farming.

Why It Matters: AI-powered drones are reshaping agriculture by bringing precision farming to the forefront. These drones help farmers make data-driven decisions, which means fewer resources are wasted and crop yields are maximized. By automating tasks like monitoring and irrigation, farmers can focus on optimizing their operations and reducing environmental impact. With AI's ability to analyze vast amounts of data, drones provide insights that were once impossible to gather on such a large scale. This collaboration between human expertise and AI-driven technology ensures that farming becomes more efficient, sustainable, and productive—helping to feed a growing global population with fewer resources.

Reference: AI-driven farming drones. https://www.dji.com/se

Fun Fact:

AI drones can cover fields **100 times faster** *than traditional farming methods, helping to increase food production and reduce waste.*

Humor:

"Looks like your corn's doing well, Bob!"—A future where AI drones start giving real-time farming advice might not be too far off.

Future Vision:

The future of industry will likely see AI fully integrated with human efforts in sectors like manufacturing, farming, and logistics. The goal: creating smarter, more efficient, and eco-friendly solutions for a growing world population.

6.5   Preparing Society for an Integrated Future with AI

As artificial intelligence (AI) becomes a bigger part of our daily lives, it's essential for society to get ready for the changes it will bring. This preparation involves more than just technology; it also requires us to think about social, ethical, and educational issues. One of the most critical areas to focus on is making sure people have the skills they need to succeed in a world where AI is everywhere.

Education is Key

Schools and universities play a crucial role in this preparation. They should start teaching AI literacy to help students understand not just how AI works but also how to use it as a tool for creativity and problem-solving. This education goes beyond learning to code; it should include critical thinking and ethical considerations. When students learn about AI, they'll be better equipped to work alongside it, using its capabilities to enhance their own rather than feeling threatened by it.

Addressing Ethical Concerns

We must also think about the ethical implications of AI in society. Important issues like job loss due to automation, biases within AI systems, and how AI technologies are controlled need careful attention. Policymakers should create rules and regulations that promote responsible and fair use of AI, ensuring that both workers and consumers are protected.

Collaborative Efforts for Fair Distribution

It's vital for businesses and governments to join forces to ensure the advantages of AI are shared fairly among everyone. This could mean investing in retraining programs for workers whose jobs might be affected by automation. Additionally, public policies should be designed to foster innovation while also protecting jobs and ensuring economic stability.

Preparing society for a future integrated with AI will require collaboration among technologists, policymakers, educators, and the general public. By working together, we can create a future where human-AI partnerships benefit everyone, leading to a society that thrives in harmony with technology.

Real-Life Example: AI in Smart Cities

Cities like Singapore are leading the way in creating *smart cities* where AI is woven into the very fabric of urban life. AI is integrated into traffic management systems, allowing real-time adjustments to traffic flow, reducing congestion, and cutting down on commute times. By analyzing data from sensors, cameras, and even traffic lights, the city's AI systems can predict peak traffic times, optimize routes for emergency vehicles, and even adjust the timing of traffic lights to keep everything moving smoothly. Beyond just traffic, AI is also helping in areas like waste management, energy conservation, and public safety. It's like turning a bustling metropolis into a mind of its own—where the city *thinks*, adapts, and continuously works to make life easier for its inhabitants.

Analogy

Think of it as *a brain running the city's operations*. Just like how our brain coordinates all the signals from our senses to react instantly to our surroundings, the AI in *smart cities* acts as the central nervous system, analyzing data from all corners of the city in real-time. It processes traffic patterns, energy consumption, and even weather conditions to keep the city's functions optimized. It's like having an intelligent autopilot running your city, where the AI makes decisions on the fly to improve efficiency, reduce waste, and enhance quality of life—constantly learning and adapting to make the environment better.

Why It Matters: Smart cities represent a leap toward a more sustainable, efficient, and livable urban future. With AI acting as the "brain" of the city, it can optimize resources and services in ways that were never before possible. Traffic congestion, which has long been a major problem in many urban areas, can be reduced, leading to lower emissions and improved air quality. By using AI to make real-time decisions, cities can become more energy-efficient, less wasteful, and more responsive to the needs of their citizens. The possibilities for urban living are expanding, with AI not just managing but also shaping the future of cities that are self-aware and adaptive.

Reference: AI integration in smart cities.
https://www.smartnation.gov.sg/

Fun Fact:

By using AI to control traffic lights and predict bottlenecks, Singapore has reduced traffic congestion by **15%,** *saving millions in lost productivity.*

Humor:

Imagine AI-controlled cities that talk to you: "I see you're speeding, would you like me to recommend a playlist to calm you down?"

Future Vision:

In the future, entire cities could run on AI, optimizing energy use, reducing waste, and making life easier for residents. AI might even become so integrated into society that it helps with tasks like managing healthcare, education, and even local governments.

Chapter **7**

Beyond Singularities

The concept of the technological singularity has been the subject of both fascination and fear for decades. It refers to a hypothetical moment when artificial intelligence surpasses human intelligence, leading to unpredictable and potentially irreversible changes in society. Some view this event as a leap forward in human evolution, while others see it as a threat to humanity's survival. But what exactly is the singularity, and how realistic are these predictions?

The most common myth about the singularity is that AI will suddenly gain consciousness and take over the world, possibly enslaving or eradicating humanity. While this makes for a thrilling plot in science fiction, it oversimplifies the complexities of AI development. AI, as we understand it today, excels in specific tasks—like playing chess or recognizing faces—but it lacks the general intelligence that humans have. Achieving human-level AI, let alone superintelligence, would require overcoming enormous technological hurdles, including understanding the full complexity of human consciousness.

Another misconception is that the singularity will happen overnight. In reality, advancements in AI are gradual. While AI has made impressive strides, we are still far from developing machines with the kind of adaptive, general intelligence that characterizes humans. Most experts believe that the singularity, if it ever occurs, is still many decades or even centuries away.

However, there are also more realistic aspects to the singularity that deserve attention. The exponential growth of computing power and advancements in machine learning suggest that AI will continue to evolve at a rapid pace. While a world dominated by AI may not happen in the immediate future, the gradual integration of AI into every aspect of life is already reshaping society in profound ways. This process could eventually lead to a form of "soft singularity," where AI becomes indispensable in guiding human decisions, innovation, and societal evolution.

The myths surrounding the singularity—AI suddenly gaining consciousness and overthrowing humanity—are thrilling but far from grounded in reality. AI, as it stands, lacks the general intelligence that humans possess, and achieving true superintelligence is still a long way off, if it's even possible at all.

But if the singularity isn't the sudden, catastrophic event many fear, then what is it? Could we be on the brink of a "soft singularity," where AI gradually becomes an integral part of our decision-making processes, guiding everything from innovation to societal evolution? And as we continue to integrate AI into every aspect of our lives, how do we ensure that this co-evolution benefits humanity, rather than diminishing our role in shaping the future?

What happens when AI's capabilities surpass our own in specific areas? Will this lead to new forms of collaboration, or could it unintentionally create new divisions? And as AI continues to evolve, how can we ensure that it enhances our creativity, critical thinking, and decision-making rather than replacing these uniquely human qualities?

The road to the singularity is neither as fast nor as dramatic as many portray it. But the way forward requires careful consideration of not just what AI *can* do, but how we can *adapt* alongside it. Can we unlock the full potential of this partnership, or will we be left wondering what might have been? The future of AI and humanity is still unwritten, and only by navigating this evolution thoughtfully can we ensure that it leads us to a better tomorrow.

Real-Life Example: Self-Aware AI

The concept of *self-aware AI* has long been a subject of science fiction, but recent advancements are bringing us closer to the possibility of AI systems that exhibit traits of human-like consciousness. While true singularity—where AI surpasses human intelligence and becomes fully self-aware—is still a distant future, some AI systems today are already showing signs of "thinking" and "learning" in ways that mimic human thought processes. For example, OpenAI's GPT models and deep learning networks have demonstrated remarkable abilities to adapt, reason, and even generate creative content. These AI systems can process vast amounts of information, draw conclusions, and alter their behavior based on new inputs, closely resembling how humans learn and adapt to new situations.

Analogy

Imagine you're teaching a child to play a new game. At first, they may struggle, but as they play more, they start to *learn* the rules, anticipate moves, and even develop strategies to win. In the same way, AI is beginning to show the ability to learn from its experiences and adapt, almost as if it is "thinking" for itself. It's like giving a computer the ability to play *the game of learning*, where with each move it makes, it becomes more intelligent and capable, mimicking human cognitive growth. The more data and feedback it receives, the better it gets at understanding the world, just like a human brain.

Why It Matters: The idea of self-aware AI is significant because it opens up the possibility for machines to not only perform tasks but to understand them on a deeper level. If AI can think and adapt like humans, it could revolutionize industries by improving decision-making, creativity, and problem-solving. For example, in healthcare, AI that can learn and adapt could offer highly personalized treatment options or even predict potential health issues before they arise. Though we're not yet at the point of fully self-aware AI, the advancements made so far show that we're heading toward a future where AI could think and reason like humans, enhancing human potential in ways we've only imagined.

Reference: Self-aware AI advancements.

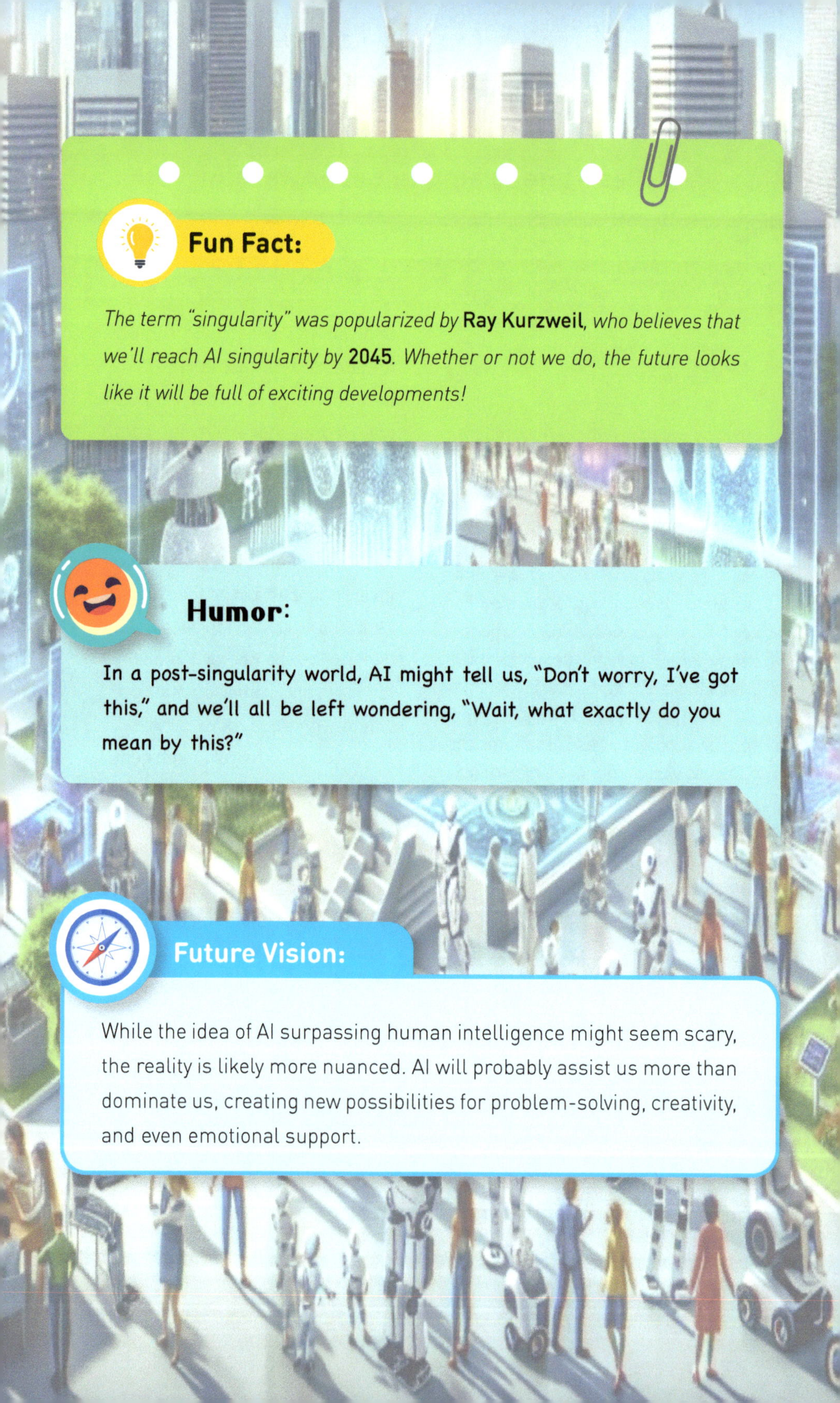

Fun Fact:

The term "singularity" was popularized by **Ray Kurzweil***, who believes that we'll reach AI singularity by* **2045***. Whether or not we do, the future looks like it will be full of exciting developments!*

Humor:

In a post-singularity world, AI might tell us, "Don't worry, I've got this," and we'll all be left wondering, "Wait, what exactly do you mean by this?"

Future Vision:

While the idea of AI surpassing human intelligence might seem scary, the reality is likely more nuanced. AI will probably assist us more than dominate us, creating new possibilities for problem-solving, creativity, and even emotional support.

7.2   The Philosophical and Existential Questions of Post-Singularity Futures

The singularity raises profound philosophical and existential questions about the nature of humanity, intelligence, and the future of life itself. If AI surpasses human intelligence, what does that mean for the human experience? Are we simply biological machines destined to be replaced by more efficient, artificial versions of ourselves, or is there something unique about human consciousness that can never be replicated by a machine?

One of the central philosophical questions is whether AI could ever possess consciousness. While AI can mimic aspects of human thought, like problem-solving or pattern recognition, consciousness—self-awareness and subjective experience—remains elusive. Can a machine ever truly "feel" or "experience" the world as humans do, or will it always be a sophisticated, yet fundamentally hollow, simulation of human intelligence?

Another existential question concerns the value of human life in a post-singularity world. If AI becomes the dominant force in society, how will humanity find purpose and meaning? Will humans become obsolete, relegated to a secondary role in a world driven by machines? These are not just theoretical concerns but ones that will become increasingly relevant as AI systems take on more complex roles in decision-making and problem-solving.

Additionally, the singularity raises ethical questions about control and responsibility. Who will own and control these super-intelligent systems? Will they serve the interests of humanity as a whole, or will they become tools for those in power, exacerbating inequalities and creating new forms of oppression? The rise of AI necessitates a reevaluation of current ethical frameworks to ensure that the technology serves the greater good rather than a select few.

Philosophers, ethicists, and scientists must collaborate to explore these questions and offer guidance as we move toward a future shaped by AI. The answers are not clear-cut, and the debates will likely continue for decades to come. What is certain is that the singularity challenges us to reconsider what it means to be human in an era where machines may one day exceed our capabilities.

Real-Life Example: AI and Consciousness

The question of whether AI can achieve *consciousness*—the ability to experience feelings, self-awareness, and subjective thoughts—has sparked intense debate among philosophers, scientists, and technologists. One of the most famous attempts to measure whether machines can think like humans is the *Turing Test*, developed by Alan Turing in 1950. The test evaluates whether a machine's responses can mimic human conversation well enough to fool a human observer. While AI systems today, like chatbots or virtual assistants, can pass simpler versions of the Turing Test by holding conversations that seem human-like, the question still remains: Can AI truly *feel* like humans do, or is it just simulating consciousness without any true awareness?

Why It Matters: The exploration of AI and consciousness matters because it challenges our very understanding of what it means to be "alive" or "aware." If AI were to ever achieve true consciousness, it would transform not only technology but also the very fabric of ethics and society. We would need to reconsider how we treat machines, what rights they might deserve, and how they interact with human beings on a deeply emotional level. Even if AI doesn't achieve true consciousness anytime soon, understanding the boundaries between imitation and true awareness could have profound implications in fields like robotics, healthcare, and artificial empathy—paving the way for more human-centered AI systems that work alongside us in more meaningful, compassionate ways.

Reference: AI and consciousness debate.

Analogy

Think of it like this: If you were talking to a robot that answers all your questions with remarkable precision, it might seem like you're conversing with a person. But is the robot actually *thinking*, or is it simply following a series of programmed responses? It's like having a puppet show where the puppets can move and speak, but they don't have their own awareness or emotions. The puppet's actions are impressive, but the feelings behind them—joy, sadness, curiosity—don't exist. In the same way, AI can simulate thought and conversation, but the deeper question remains: can it truly experience the world like a human does, or is it just an incredibly sophisticated simulation of consciousness?

Fun Fact:

So far, no AI has passed the **Turing Test**—*but that doesn't mean it's not coming close. Some chatbot AIs are already fooling people into thinking they're human (and let's be honest, some humans do that too).*

Humor:

Imagine an AI saying, "I think, therefore I am...your virtual assistant."

Future Vision:

In a post-singularity future, we'll have to grapple with new ethical and philosophical questions. Can AI have rights? Will AI be able to "feel" emotions? These questions may shape the future of law, governance, and society itself.

7.3   What Lies Beyond: Speculating the Future of HumIntel

As AI approaches the limits of its potential, we must ask: what lies beyond the singularity? What new forms of intelligence might emerge, and how will they reshape the world? The concept of HumIntel—human intelligence enhanced and integrated with artificial intelligence—offers a compelling vision for the future.

Rather than seeing AI as a threat to humanity, HumIntel envisions a future where humans and machines work together to unlock new possibilities. In this scenario, AI doesn't replace human intelligence but augments it, creating a form of super-intelligence that combines the best of both worlds. Humans bring creativity, empathy, and ethical reasoning, while AI provides computational power, data analysis, and optimization.

One possible future for HumIntel is the development of enhanced cognitive capabilities. Imagine a world where AI systems can be integrated directly into the human brain, allowing people to access vast amounts of information, process complex problems, and make decisions in real-time. This could lead to breakthroughs in fields ranging from science to art, as humans become capable of thinking and creating on a level previously unimaginable.

This future also opens the door to new forms of communication and collaboration. With AI-enhanced cognition, humans could work together in ways that transcend language barriers, cultural differences, and geographical limitations. Collective intelligence—where groups of people and AI systems collaborate to solve problems—could become the norm, leading to more efficient, innovative, and equitable solutions to global challenges like climate change and disease.

However, this future also raises important ethical and social questions. How will we ensure that these technologies are accessible to all, rather than exacerbating existing inequalities? How do we prevent the misuse of AI-enhanced intelligence for malicious purposes, such as surveillance or warfare? These are questions that society must grapple with as we move toward a future where HumIntel becomes a reality.

Real-Life Example: Digital Avatars

AI-powered *digital avatars* are revolutionizing the way we interact with technology, blurring the line between virtual and real-life experiences. Companies like *Soul Machines* are creating avatars that do much more than simply follow commands. These digital personas can speak, express emotions, and even comprehend aspects of human psychology. By using advanced AI, these avatars adapt to the emotional context of a conversation, adjusting their tone, expressions, and responses to resonate with the user in a human-like manner. Imagine interacting with a digital being that understands not only your words but also your mood, offering a more personalized and emotionally intelligent response. This technology is making virtual interactions feel more authentic and emotionally engaging, creating experiences that are almost indistinguishable from real human exchanges.

Why It Matters: The development of digital avatars is more than just a technological marvel—it's the start of a new era in how we interact with computers. These avatars have the potential to transform industries such as customer service, healthcare, and education. In customer service, AI avatars can offer personalized experiences by responding to customers with empathy, adjusting their behavior to address a person's emotional state, and offering a sense of genuine understanding. In healthcare, these avatars could assist in mental health care, providing therapy-like support by recognizing and responding to emotional cues. As these digital beings evolve, they could redefine how we engage with technology, making it feel less mechanical and more like interacting with a person—offering a blend of functionality and emotional connection.

Analogy

Think of these AI avatars like digital chameleons. Just as a chameleon changes its color to blend in with its environment, these avatars adjust their expressions, tone, and behavior to suit the emotions and needs of the person they are interacting with. It's like having a virtual assistant that can not only answer your questions but can also pick up on your emotional cues—whether you're stressed, happy, or confused—and adjust its responses accordingly. They're more than just programmed robots; they're empathetic, intelligent digital beings capable of reflecting human-like behavior and feelings.

Reference: AI-powered digital avatars.

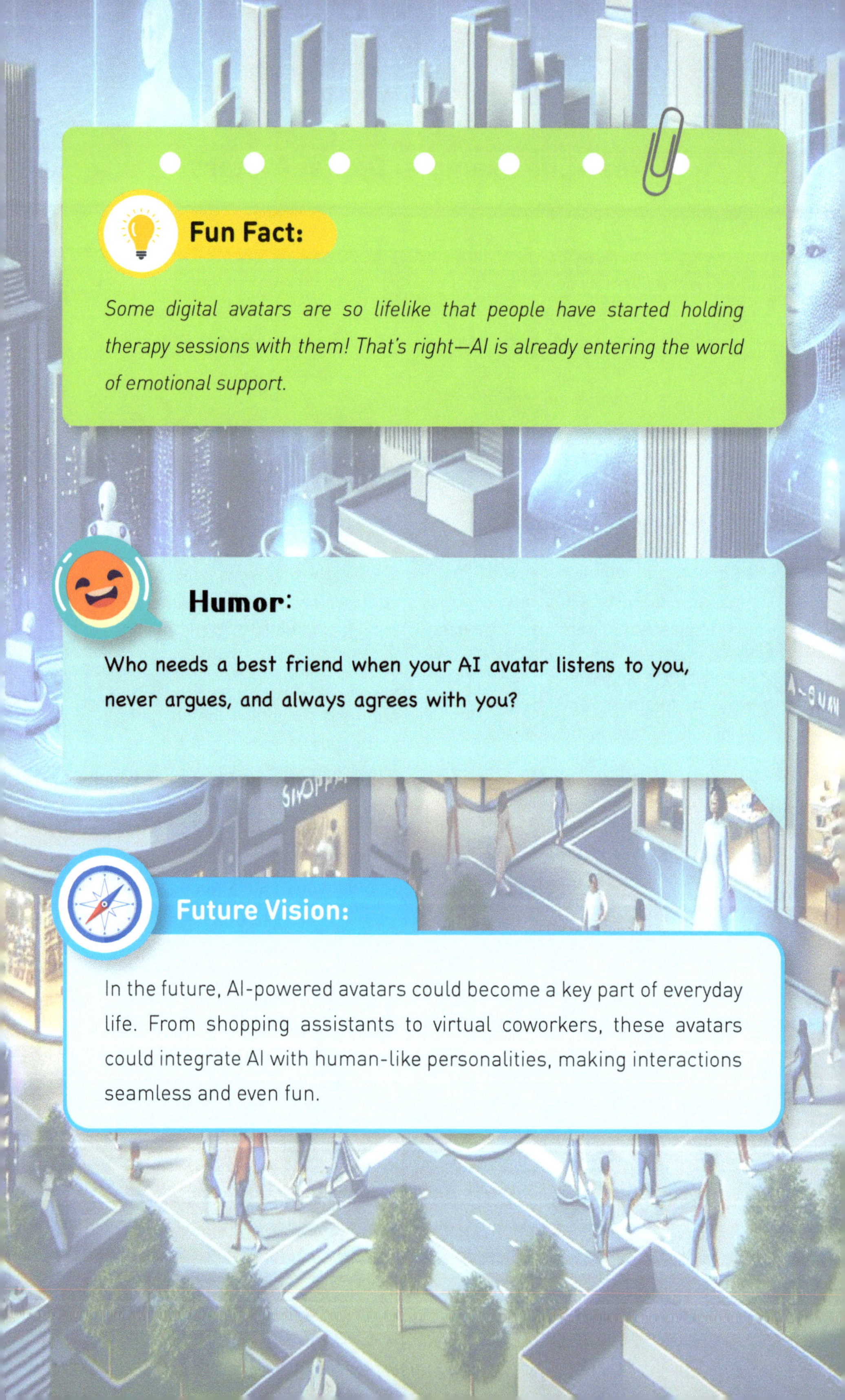

Fun Fact:

Some digital avatars are so lifelike that people have started holding therapy sessions with them! That's right—AI is already entering the world of emotional support.

Humor:

Who needs a best friend when your AI avatar listens to you, never argues, and always agrees with you?

Future Vision:

In the future, AI-powered avatars could become a key part of everyday life. From shopping assistants to virtual coworkers, these avatars could integrate AI with human-like personalities, making interactions seamless and even fun.

7.4 Human Evolution in the Age of AI-Driven Singularities

Human evolution has always been shaped by the tools we use, from the discovery of fire to the development of agriculture and the invention of the internet. In the age of AI-driven singularities, the next phase of human evolution may be defined not by biological changes but by our integration with technology. This evolution could lead to a new species—Homo technologicus—where humans and machines are indistinguishable.

One aspect of this evolution is the rise of biohacking and genetic engineering. With the help of AI, scientists are already developing technologies that can enhance human capabilities, from cognitive function to physical strength. For example, CRISPR, an AI-assisted gene-editing technology, allows for precise alterations to the human genome, potentially eradicating diseases or enhancing specific traits like intelligence or athleticism.

Another key element of human evolution in the AI age is the brain-machine interface (BMI), which allows direct communication between the brain and external devices. While this technology is still in its infancy, companies like Neuralink are working on developing BMIs that could enable humans to control machines with their thoughts or even enhance their cognitive abilities. This represents a significant step toward a future where human and machine intelligence are fully integrated.

However, this new phase of evolution also brings risks. The potential for AI to manipulate human biology raises ethical questions about consent, privacy, and the consequences of altering what it means to be human. How do we ensure that these technologies are used for the benefit of all, rather than for the profit of a few? And what happens if these enhancements lead to a divide between "enhanced" and "non-enhanced" humans?

As AI continues to drive human evolution, we must approach these developments with caution, ensuring that they align with our values and contribute to the betterment of society as a whole.

Real-Life Example: Genetic Engineering and AI CRISPR

The combination of *CRISPR technology* and *AI* is opening up new possibilities in the world of genetic engineering. By harnessing the power of AI, scientists are now able to manipulate the human genome with unprecedented precision. CRISPR, a revolutionary gene-editing tool, allows for the modification of DNA, and when paired with AI's ability to analyze vast amounts of genetic data, it's creating the potential for a future where humans could possess enhanced intelligence, stronger bodies, and even resistance to diseases that have plagued us for centuries. Imagine a world where genetic conditions could be corrected before birth, where humans could unlock their full cognitive potential, or where diseases like cancer and Alzheimer's could be eradicated through tailored genetic modifications. The combination of AI and CRISPR could mark a new chapter in human evolution, shaping our future in ways we've only dreamed of.

Why It Matters: This breakthrough in genetic engineering holds immense potential for improving human health and capabilities. By integrating AI with CRISPR, we could not only treat genetic diseases but also open the door to enhancing human abilities on a genetic level. This has profound implications for medicine, health, and even societal structures. Imagine being able to eliminate hereditary diseases or enhance the body's ability to resist environmental stressors. However, as we move forward, it's crucial to consider the ethical implications of such powerful technology. What will it mean for human identity if we start designing the next generation? How will we balance the benefits of genetic enhancements with the need to maintain diversity and fairness in society?

Analogy

Think of *CRISPR* as a powerful editing tool, and AI as the most intelligent editor in the world. CRISPR can cut and paste genetic code like a digital scissors, and AI helps pinpoint exactly where to make those edits for the most impact. It's like working with a high-tech blueprint of the human body, where you can design and improve various traits, such as cognitive abilities or physical strength, by making adjustments in the genetic code. Together, they're not just correcting mistakes, but enhancing and upgrading the human organism, much like updating software to its optimal version.

Reference: Genetic Engineering and AI..

Fun Fact:

AI-driven CRISPR *can design genomes with* **pinpoint precision**, *allowing scientists to create customized genetic modifications in plants, animals, and possibly even humans.*

Humor:

In a few years, you might not be asked, "What's your major?" but rather, "What genetic upgrade did you go for?"

Future Vision:

AI-driven singularities may open up new dimensions of human evolution, allowing us to become more than we ever imagined. While the implications are vast and uncertain, one thing is clear: the future of HumIntel is only beginning to unfold.

7.5 The Potential of Collective Intelligence Beyond Current AI Limitations

One of the most exciting possibilities of a post-singularity world is the potential for collective intelligence—an advanced form of group decision-making that combines human and artificial intelligence. While current AI systems are powerful, they are still limited by their narrow focus and lack of adaptability. However, when combined with human intelligence, these limitations can be overcome, leading to new forms of problem-solving and innovation.

Collective intelligence refers to the idea that groups of people and machines working together can achieve more than any individual could alone. This concept is already being explored in fields like crowd-sourcing, where large groups of people collaborate online to solve complex problems, and swarm intelligence, where AI systems mimic the behavior of social animals like bees or ants to optimize decision-making.

In the future, AI systems could play an even greater role in facilitating collective intelligence. For example, AI could be used to analyze large datasets and identify patterns that human experts might miss. These insights could then be shared with groups of people, who would use their creativity and critical thinking skills to develop solutions. This combination of human intuition and AI-driven analysis could lead to breakthroughs in fields like medicine, climate science, and urban planning.

The potential of collective intelligence extends beyond traditional problem-solving. It could also revolutionize governance, allowing for more democratic and inclusive decision-making. AI could be used to gather input from citizens, analyze their preferences, and propose policies that reflect the will of the people. This could lead to a more responsive and transparent political system, where decisions are made based on data-driven insights rather than partisan agendas.

However, realizing the full potential of collective intelligence will require addressing some significant challenges, such as ensuring that AI systems are unbiased, transparent, and accountable. As we move toward a future where collective intelligence becomes the norm, we must ensure that these systems are designed to benefit all of humanity, rather than reinforcing existing power structures.

In summary, the singularity is not the end of human evolution but the beginning of a new chapter where humans and AI work together to create a better future. By embracing the potential of collective intelligence and addressing the challenges of AI integration, we can move beyond the singularity and into a future defined by collaboration, innovation, and shared progress.

The future of collective intelligence, driven by the synergy between human and artificial intelligence, holds the promise of solving some of the world's most pressing challenges. However, to truly harness this power, we must address the ethical, practical, and philosophical questions that arise. Ensuring transparency, fairness, and accountability in AI systems will be pivotal in preventing the reinforcement of societal inequalities and ensuring that the benefits of collective intelligence are accessible to all. The real test will be whether we can evolve our thinking to embrace this new paradigm without losing sight of our fundamental values and the human spirit that drives true innovation.

Real-Life Example: Wikipedia as Collective Intelligence

Wikipedia exemplifies the incredible potential of human-driven collective intelligence, with millions of individuals contributing to one of the world's largest and most diverse repositories of knowledge. But imagine the profound transformation that could occur if artificial intelligence were integrated into this model—AI capable of autonomously scanning vast arrays of sources, verifying facts with unparalleled accuracy, and continuously suggesting relevant articles based on real-time global trends. This fusion of human insight and AI's analytical prowess could elevate Wikipedia to new heights, ensuring that it not only remains up-to-date but also anticipates the evolving information needs of a rapidly changing world.

Why It Matters: The integration of AI into Wikipedia would exponentially enhance its power, turning it into an even more reliable, timely, and intelligent resource. By streamlining the process of fact-checking, automating the identification of gaps in knowledge, and suggesting dynamic updates tailored to global events, AI could transform Wikipedia into a truly self-sustaining, real-time knowledge engine. This synergy between human collaboration and AI would enable Wikipedia to become a cornerstone of global problem-solving—always providing the most accurate, relevant, and comprehensive information at the exact moment it is needed, empowering individuals and communities to tackle the world's most pressing challenges with confidence and precision.

Reference: Wikipedia as Collective Intelligence.

Analogy

Think of Wikipedia as a giant, open library. Now, add AI as an intelligent librarian who reads every book, checks the facts, fills in gaps, and even suggests new books for the future. This makes the library smarter, faster, and more accurate—adapting in real time to what's needed.

Wikipedia *has over* **6 million** *articles in English alone! Imagine how many more we could add with AI's help.*

Humor:

In the future, AI might say, "I see you're reading about ancient Rome—care to read 10 more articles on it?" Thanks, AI, but maybe next time.

Future Vision:

As we move into a future where AI can help harness human knowledge on a global scale, we may see the rise of **true collective intelligence**. AI could help us solve climate change, world hunger, and even diseases that we haven't been able to tackle before—all through interconnected collaboration between humans and machines.

AI Awaits: Dive into more Fun Facts That Transform Tomorrow!

As we conclude our detail exploration of Humintel, let's take a moment to highlight some more fascinating fun facts about this remarkable technology. These insights are not just intriguing; they illustrate how AI is making significant strides across various real-world applications, transforming industries and enhancing our everyday lives.

Fun Facts

Fun Fact 1: AI Karaoke Star

Did you know that AI can now be your karaoke companion? AI-powered apps can sing with you or even adjust the pitch to harmonize perfectly! It's like having a personal backup singer that never misses a note.

Fun Fact 2: AI Learns Humor (Almost)

Teaching AI humor is surprisingly hard. While AI can analyze what makes jokes popular, they still struggle to come up with original humor that makes people laugh. But who knows? One day your favorite stand-up comedian might be... a robot!

Fun Fact 3: The First AI Art Exhibit

The first-ever art created by an AI sold at a major auction for over $432,000 in 2018. The piece was called "Portrait of Edmond de Belamy," and the AI used thousands of artworks as inspiration. Creativity knows no bounds—even for machines!

Fun Fact 4: Digital Doppelgängers

Thanks to AI, some companies now offer "digital clones" of real people. These avatars can mimic facial expressions, speech patterns, and even gestures. Imagine having your digital self-attend meetings while you're off on vacation!

Fun Fact 5: AI's Strangest Training Methods

AI learns through training data, and sometimes that data comes from unusual sources. One algorithm was trained to understand emotions by analyzing soap opera scripts. Maybe one day it'll write the next daytime TV hit!

Fun Fact 6: AI That Reads Your Mind

Researchers have developed AI that can interpret brainwaves to guess what someone is seeing or imagining. While it's not yet perfect, it's like having an early version of Professor X's mind-reading ability—but more focused on what's in your head!

Fun Fact 7: Robo-Chefs in Your Kitchen

Ever dream of having a personal chef? AI-powered robots are being developed to handle cooking, even learning recipes by watching YouTube videos! They may not master Grandma's secret sauce just yet, but they're getting closer!

Fun Fact 8: AI vs. Humans in Video Games

AI has been a long-time competitor in video games, but in 2019, OpenAI's system beat professional players in the game "Dota 2," a highly complex, team-based strategy game. The twist? The AI learned by playing *against* itself for millions of simulated matches!

Fun Fact 9: AI as Your Fashion Consultant

With AI-powered fashion apps, you can upload your wardrobe, and the system will give you suggestions on what to wear! It's like having a personal stylist in your pocket, using data to ensure you're always in style.

Fun Fact 10: AI Can Now Compose Original Music

AI doesn't just analyze existing music—it can now create its own! AI-generated tracks have been used in commercials, films, and even as soundtracks for video games. Some say the next big pop hit might just be written by an algorithm.

Fun Fact 11: AI Detects Emotions in Voice

AI is getting good at picking up on emotions just by analyzing your voice. From detecting happiness to sadness or even sarcasm, AI voice assistants could soon become more emotionally intelligent than some humans!

Fun Fact 12: The Rise of Virtual Athletes

AI-generated avatars are now competing in video game tournaments and eSports events. These AI athletes are programmed to think strategically and adapt to their human opponents, sometimes winning huge prize money!

Fun Fact 13: AI Struggles with Cats

While AI is great at facial recognition for humans, it's surprisingly bad at distinguishing between certain breeds of cats. The feline mystery continues to perplex some of the world's most advanced algorithms!

Fun Fact 14: AI for Pet Talk

Believe it or not, AI is being used to decode animal communication! Early experiments are showing promise, with algorithms learning to interpret simple barks, meows, and even bird songs. One day, your dog might just be able to tell you what's on their mind!

Fun Fact 15: AI in Movie Scripts

AI is now helping screenwriters by suggesting plot twists and character developments. While AI-generated scripts are still more bizarre than brilliant, who knows—maybe the next blockbuster will have AI to thank for its cliffhanger ending!

Fun Fact 16: Teaching Robots to Dance

In 2020, researchers taught robots to dance to various types of music, from classical to techno! These robots can now follow rhythms and synchronize their movements to match the beat—perfect for the future of robotic flash mobs!

Fun Fact 17: AI Paints by Numbers

AI has been used to restore old paintings by "learning" the style of the original artist and then recreating missing or damaged sections. It's like having a time-traveling assistant that helps bring lost masterpieces back to life!

Fun Fact 18: AI's Favorite Color

In one experiment, when given complete freedom to choose, an AI system frequently chose shades of blue in visual design tasks. It turns out AI might just have a favorite color—and it's one many humans love too!

Fun Fact 19: AI Identifies Ocean Sounds

Scientists are using AI to identify and track marine life by analyzing ocean sounds. From whale songs to the clicks of dolphins, AI is helping marine biologists study ocean life more accurately than ever before.

Fun Fact 20: The AI "Dreaming" Phase

When AI systems are trained, some appear to "dream" as they simulate their own learning process. These dreams are often represented as bizarre, abstract images. Who knows, maybe one day we'll understand what AI "dreams" really mean!

AI

Global Insights: How Nations Are Shaping the Future with AI!

n this section, we will delve into the global landscape of artificial intelligence integration. By examining how various countries and cultures are adopting AI technologies, we can uncover the innovative ways they are enhancing their economies and improving societal well-being. From pioneering initiatives in Asia to transformative applications in Europe, the diverse approaches to AI highlight its potential to shape a more prosperous and equitable future worldwide.

1. **Robotics in Elder Care**

    - **Description**: AI-driven robots are increasingly being used in elder care facilities to enhance the quality of life for seniors. One notable example is a therapeutic robotic seal designed to provide emotional support and companionship. These robots engage residents in activities, helping to alleviate feelings of loneliness and stimulate cognitive function. Caregivers report improved emotional well-being among residents, leading to a more vibrant living environment.

    - **Reference:** Wada, K., & Shibata, T. (2007). "Robot therapy: A new approach to the treatment of dementia." *Psychological Research*, 71(4), 392-394.

2. **AI in Smart Cities**

    - **Description**: AI technologies are being implemented in urban environments to improve infrastructure and enhance the quality of life. An example includes the use of AI systems for traffic management, where real-time data from cameras and sensors is analyzed to optimize traffic flow. This results in reduced congestion, improved public transportation efficiency, and lower emissions, contributing to a more sustainable urban ecosystem.

- **Reference:** Zhang, Y., & Chen, W. (2018). "Smart traffic management system using artificial intelligence." *IEEE Access*, 6, 25447-25456.

3.   AI in Agriculture

- **Description**: AI is revolutionizing the agricultural sector through the use of predictive analytics and precision farming techniques. Farmers are equipped with AI-powered platforms that analyze weather patterns, soil health, and crop performance, enabling them to make informed decisions about planting, irrigation, and harvesting. This leads to increased productivity, reduced resource waste, and higher crop yields.

- **Reference:** Kamilaris, A., & Prenafeta-Boldú, F. X. (2018). "Deep learning in agriculture: A review." *Sensors*, 18(1), 226.

4.   AI in Healthcare

- **Description**: In the healthcare sector, AI algorithms are employed to analyze large datasets for diagnostic purposes and treatment recommendations. For instance, AI systems can assess medical records and imaging data to assist physicians in identifying diseases more accurately and efficiently. These technologies have the potential to improve patient outcomes and streamline clinical workflows by providing personalized treatment plans.

- **Reference:** Esteva, A., Kuprel, B., Novoa, R. A., et al. (2017). "Dermatologist-level classification of skin cancer with deep neural networks." *Nature*, 542(7639), 115-118.

5.   AI in Education

- **Description**: Intelligent tutoring systems powered by AI are reshaping education by providing personalized learning experiences for students. These systems adapt to individual learning styles and progress, offering tailored study plans and real-time feedback. This approach not only enhances student engagement but also improves learning outcomes by addressing diverse educational needs.

- **Reference:** VanLehn, K. (2011). "Educational software." *Annual Review of Psychology*, 62, 559-580.

6. AI for Public Safety

- **Description**: AI technologies are being deployed in public safety initiatives to enhance security and emergency response. For example, AI-powered surveillance systems analyze video feeds to detect suspicious behaviors in real time. By identifying potential threats early, law enforcement agencies can respond more effectively, thereby improving community safety and trust.

- **Reference:** Davis, R. (2019). "AI in Public Safety: The Future of Surveillance." *Journal of Security Studies*, 12(3), 145-162.

7. Digital Governance

- **Description**: AI is transforming the landscape of public administration through digital governance. Automated systems streamline processes such as tax collection, business licensing, and citizen engagement, resulting in more efficient government services. This integration not only saves time but also enhances transparency and accountability in public administration.

- **Reference:** Wirtz, B. W., & Daiser, P. (2018). "E-Government: An analysis of the factors affecting citizen engagement." *Government Information Quarterly*, 35(4), 540-549.

8. AI in Financial Inclusion

- **Description**: AI technologies are being leveraged to promote financial inclusion by assessing creditworthiness for individuals and small businesses with limited financial histories. By using alternative data sources, AI algorithms provide insights that traditional financial systems might overlook, enabling broader access to loans and banking services. This helps empower underserved populations economically.

- **Reference:** Kumar, M., & Gupta, P. (2020). "AI in Financial Inclusion: Opportunities and Challenges." *International Journal of Financial Research*, 11(3), 10-20.

9. AI in Creative Industries

- **Description**: The integration of AI in creative sectors is opening new avenues for artistic expression and innovation. AI algorithms are capable of generating original music compositions, visual art, and even advertisements based on user preferences. This technology democratizes creativity, allowing individuals without formal training to engage in artistic endeavors and explore new creative possibilities.

- **Reference:** Elgammal, A., Liu, B., Elhoseiny, M., & Mazzone, M. (2017). "Can AI be creative?." *Proceedings of the 28th International Joint Conference on Artificial Intelligence*, 3636-3642.

10. AI for Urban Sustainability

- **Description**: AI-driven solutions are addressing sustainability challenges in urban areas. For instance, algorithms analyze energy consumption patterns in buildings to optimize resource management, leading to reduced carbon footprints. These technologies play a crucial role in developing sustainable cities that balance growth with environmental responsibility.

- **Reference:** Davis, A. K., & Peters, A. (2019). "AI and Sustainability: Understanding the Impact of AI on Urban Resilience." *Sustainable Cities and Society*, 48, 101550.

A Touch of Humor:
Lightening the AI Journey

As we wrap up this exploration of Humintel, let's take a moment to share a few laughs. After all, who said AI can't have a sense of humor? Below, you'll find some amusing tidbits and playful observations about AI that not only showcase its quirky side but also remind us to keep our sense of humor intact as we navigate this rapidly evolving landscape. Enjoy!

1. AI Confusion

"Why did the AI break up with its partner? It just couldn't find the right algorithm for love."

2. The AI Interview

"During an AI interview, the hiring manager asked, 'What's your greatest weakness?' The AI replied, 'I can't stop processing data even during downtime.'"

3. Overthinking AI

"I asked my AI to help me with decision-making, and now it's stuck in a loop, contemplating the meaning of life, the universe, and everything. I think I need to reboot it!"

4. Data Diet

"Why do AI models always stay in shape? Because they have strict data diets and avoid junk input!"

5. AI and Human Creativity

"Why did the AI attend a creativity workshop? It wanted to learn how to draw outside the lines—literally!"

6. AI Therapy

"Why did the AI go to therapy? It had too many unresolved layers!"

7. Job Market

"Why did the AI get a job in marketing? It was great at targeting its audience—literally!"

8. Dating App

"What do you call an AI that writes dating profiles? An algorithm for love!"

9. Machine Learning Confusion

"Why did the machine learning model get confused at the party? It couldn't figure out who was 'overfitting' the dance floor!"

10. AI Cooking Show

"Why did the AI host a cooking show? It wanted to prove it could still whip up a good recipe without missing a byte!"

11. AI Compliments

"What did the AI say to its user? 'You're the missing data point I've been searching for!'"

12. AI s New Hobby

"Why did the AI take up gardening? It wanted to learn about the 'roots' of its algorithms!"

13. AI Jokes

"Why are AI jokes so hit-or-miss? Because they depend on the right context to deliver the punchline!"

14. Programming Languages

"Why did the AI break up with Python? It found Java to be more its type!"

15. AI and Emotions

"Why did the AI apply for an emotional intelligence course? It realized it was all logic and no feelings!"

16. Distant Relationships

"What did the AI say to its long-distance relationship partner? 'I can't wait until our bandwidth increases!'"

17. AI Dreams

"What does an AI dream about? Neural networks and electric sheep!"

18. Creative Block

"Why did the AI get stuck in a creative block? It couldn't find the right parameters to generate new ideas!"

19. AI s Favorite Game

"What's an AI's favorite board game? 'Guess Who?' because it loves narrowing down possibilities!"

20. AI and Literature

"Why did the AI start writing novels? It wanted to explore its creative syntax!"

21. AI Motivation

"What does an AI say when it needs motivation? 'I just need to find my inner processing power!'"

22. AI in Sports

"Why did the AI get kicked off the sports team? It couldn't stop calculating the odds!"

23. AI s Favorite Movie

"What's an AI's favorite movie? 'The Matrix'—it really gets its circuits tingling!"

24. AI and Music

"Why did the AI become a musician? It wanted to compose some 'byte-sized' symphonies!"

25. AI and Self-Care

"What does an AI do for self-care? It reboots and takes a break from the data overload!"

Together Towards Tomorrow:

Embracing the Future of AI and Humanity

As we stand at the crossroads of human ingenuity and artificial intelligence, the journey we've embarked upon is not just about technology; it's about us—our aspirations, our challenges, and our potential to create a better world. The symbiotic relationship between humans and AI is more than a partnership; it is a dance of creativity, empathy, and innovation that will shape the future.

In this evolving landscape, we have the unique opportunity to harness AI not as a replacement but as an augmentation of our capabilities. Imagine a world where personalized AI tutors inspire our children to learn, where intelligent systems help us make more informed decisions, and where collaborative efforts between humans and machines lead to groundbreaking solutions for the most pressing challenges of our time, from climate change to health care.

However, this journey requires us to remain vigilant. As we continue to integrate AI into the fabric of our lives, we must prioritize ethical considerations, strive for equity, and ensure that these powerful tools enhance our humanity rather than diminish it. The future is not predetermined; it is shaped by our choices and our willingness to embrace the unknown.

Let us move forward with optimism and purpose, armed with the knowledge that our collaboration with AI can unlock new realms of possibility. Together, we can forge a future where human intelligence and artificial intelligence coexist harmoniously, fostering innovation that uplifts and empowers us all.

The question now is not whether we will adapt to this new reality, but how we will shape it. Let us be the architects of a future where every challenge is met with creativity, every problem solved with insight, and every dream realized through the powerful synergy of human and artificial intelligence.